PILGRIM WALKS

IN FRANCISCAN ITALY

AND OTHER SELECTED WRITINGS

JOHANNES JØRGENSEN

Honorary citizen of Assisi;
five times nominated for the Nobel Prize in Literature

EDITED AND INTRODUCED BY JON M. SWEENEY

San Damiano Books

PARACLETE PRESS
BREWSTER, MASSACHUSETTS

2020 First Printing

Pilgrim Walks in Franciscan Italy: And Other Selected Writings

Copyright © 2020 Jon M. Sweeney

ISBN 978-1-64060-345-5

All quotations from Holy Scripture are rendered in the Douay-Rheims 1899
American Edition.

The Paraclete Press name and logo (dove on cross) and the San Damiano Books logo
are trademarks of Paraclete Press, Inc.

  Library of Congress Cataloging-in-Publication Data
Names: Jørgensen, Johannes, 1866-1956, author. | Sweeney, Jon M., 1967-
    editor.
Title: Pilgrim walks in Franciscan Italy : and other selected writings /
    Johannes Jorgensen ; edited and introduced by Jon M. Sweeney.
Description: Brewster, Massachusetts : San Damiano Books, Paraclete Press,
    2020. | Summary: "Jørgensen describes a pilgrimage to places in Italy
    that were dear to Francis and his early companions and offers
    inspiration to all who seek to follow the way of St. Francis today"--
    Provided by publisher.
Identifiers: LCCN 2020015883 (print) | LCCN 2020015884 (ebook) | ISBN
    9781640603455 (trade paperback) | ISBN 9781640603462 (mobi) | ISBN
    9781640603479 (epub) | ISBN 9781640603486 (pdf)
Subjects: LCSH: Christian pilgrims and pilgrimages--Italy. | Francis, of
    Assisi, Saint, 1182-1226. | Catherine, of Siena, Saint, 1347-1380.
Classification: LCC BX2320.5.I8 J665 2020 (print) | LCC BX2320.5.I8
    (ebook) | DDC 263/.04245--dc23
LC record available at https://lccn.loc.gov/2020015883
LC ebook record available at https://lccn.loc.gov/2020015884

10 9 8 7 6 5 4 3 2 1

Published by Paraclete Press
Brewster, Massachusetts
www.paracletepress.com

Printed in the United States of America

CONTENTS

INTRODUCTION

*T*HERE IS NO BOOK QUITE LIKE THIS ONE IF YOU know a little bit about St. Francis of Assisi and want to know more. Each chapter of Part One describes a pilgrimage to a place in Italy that's central to Francis's biography, written by one of his most literary modern biographers. These places in Umbria, Tuscany, and Lazio were dear to Francis and his early companions—those who were persecuted after the saint's death for daring to follow his example of poverty literally. As a recent Italian biographer of St. Francis, Chiari Mercuri, has written:

> Poggio Bustone, La Foresta, Monteripido, Sarteano, Sefro, La Verna, Fonte Colombo, Greccio, Cantalice, Monteluco became the living places of the companions, who were now dispersed and split up. These hermitages, during the periods of persecution—as under the generalship of Bonaventure . . . were transformed into places of Franciscan dissent and resistance, carried on, however, always in secret and in the privacy of their own cells, "without creating disputes or questions," as Francis had recommended to them.[1]

---

1 Chiara Mercuri, *Francis of Assisi: The Hidden Story*, trans. Robert J. Edmonson (Brewster, MA: Paraclete Press, 2019), 164.

Johannes Jørgensen brings these places to life. His descriptions capture holy places as they presented themselves to his senses a little more than a century ago. It's a glimpse of a bygone world and an inspiration to all who seek to follow the way of St. Francis today. The author knows how to paint a picture and make you feel that you are there in that place. For example, in chapter 8 he describes what he sees and feels walking into Cortona looking for the Convent of Le Celle ("the cells") where Francis lived probably in 1211:

> Soon after midday I set out for Celle. It is one of the very oldest settlements of the Franciscan Order. The day was warm. A hot haze brooded over the wide valley of Chiesa, marked out as it was into vineyards, dotted with cypresses, intersected by white roads. Blue mountains rose in the distance. I heard the cuckoo's cry, and happy butterflies flitted past me.

Before Cortona, it's no accident that Jørgensen begins his pilgrimage in the town of Greccio. He writes while he's there:

> As I knelt amid those barefooted, brown-habited friars, who in the darkness raised their hands and their hearts to heaven in voiceless prayer, I realized more vividly than ever before what the Middle Ages were— how far removed the twentieth century was—how far away beyond the crest of the mountains was the modern world, and how remote the great, busy towns, with their glare and noise, unrest and endless amusements, seemed.

Greccio is where Francis performed one of his softer miracles of humanism and joy—creating the world's first live Nativity scene—and it is the place Blessed John of Parma chose for his mandatory retreat and silence after being condemned by Bonaventure for overseeing a chaotic time in the Order after Francis's death. These are characters whom you will meet more deliberately in the pages to follow. Greccio was a place of intense isolation, and Jørgensen writes of John of Parma with reverence and prayer.

Francis of Assisi hasn't always been the world's most popular saint. A renaissance of Franciscan spirituality began in the late nineteenth century when a French pastor-scholar, Paul Sabatier, wrote the first modern biography of Francis. Sabatier hunted for original sources all over Italy and throughout the monasteries and friaries of Europe. His work was published in French in 1893. A year later the book appeared in English and was also prominently placed on The Index of Forbidden Books, then maintained by the Roman Catholic Church, because the book dared to question some of the overly simple assumptions that had long been promulgated by the hagiographical tradition. In fact, the Index's tag practically insured the book's success. Within a few years, Sabatier's work was translated into many languages, and the appeal of St. Francis quickly grew into the twentieth century. This fervor continued through 1926, the 700th anniversary of Francis's death—which was celebrated throughout the world—and has continued largely unabated into the twenty-first century.

Jørgensen's great biography of Francis fell within the time of early fervor, and the Dane wrote several other interesting books besides. One of those others is what you find complete here as Part One: *Pilgrim Walks in Franciscan Italy*. Short selections from several others comprise Part Two.

Jørgensen was part of a Catholic literary revival that saw books by Catholics flourish and renowned writers convert to Catholicism. This period began at the same time as the renaissance around St. Francis started, near the end of the nineteenth century, and it continued through the first three decades of the twentieth. It featured names such as Péguy, Claudel, Bloy, Huysmans, and Maritain in pre-World War I France, followed by Mauriac and Bernanos after the epoch-changing tragedy of the trenches. In England, there were waves, from John Henry Newman and Gerard Manley Hopkins, to G. K. Chesterton and Hilaire Belloc on the road to Rome, followed by Evelyn Waugh and Graham Greene. In Norway, there was the great Sigrid Undset, and in Germany, the Jewish philosopher and Catholic convert Edith Stein. The Catholic literary revival arrived later to the United States, with people such as Dorothy Day and Thomas Merton in the 1930s and 1940s. The Danish Johannes Jørgensen's career spans all this time.

He was an outspoken convert, received into the Catholic Church after many years of fighting with it. Baptized as a Lutheran with the name Johannes (John), in honor of St. John the Baptist, after becoming Catholic he wrote that he knew that, "in spite of all unworthiness, in spite of all weakness, I was to be like him, a voice crying in the wilderness, and one who was to prepare the way of the Highest."[2] He would go on to research and write the lives of saints.

Jørgensen's work exerted an influence on Dorothy Day through Peter Maurin; together, these two founded the Catholic Worker movement. Maurin often spoke of Jørgensen's work, most of all his biography of St. Francis. This is the book of Jørgensen's that has, by far, exerted the greatest influence. Maurin even wrote sixteen lines of verse about Jørgensen's *Saint Francis of Assisi* and the image it portrayed of the saint giving up his possessions, working with his hands, offering his talents as a service to others, receiving help from others as well as giving it, and going through life giving thanks to God.[3]

Among Jørgensen's other books on the saints are his biographies of Catherine of Siena and Bridget of Sweden. These works, too, involved much travel and original research. They were also widely appreciated. One reviewer in *Studies: An Irish Quarterly Review*, published by the Jesuits in Ireland, described those works very well in 1938. I cannot improve on this description of Jørgensen's work except to say we should replace the word "hagiography" with "saint biography"— because "hagiography" once meant, simply, writing the lives of saints, but today it carries negative connotations:

2 Johannes Jørgensen, *An Autobiography,* trans. Ingeborg Lund, vol. 1, (London: Sheed & Ward, 1928), 201.
3 See *A Revolution of the Heart: Essays on the Catholic Worker,* ed. Patrick G. Coy (Philadelphia: Temple University Press, 1988), 19.

This is hagiography [saint biography] as it ought to be written. It lives! Johannes Jorgensen is no smug preacher weaving a weary sermon around the *"gesta Dei per Catherinam"* or dull industrious scholar comparing texts for muck-raking historians to utilize and psychologists to abuse. He is a poet, a maker as much as a student. He makes us see! . . . We are no longer in chairs of modern comfort before neat electric radiators; we are loafing in the streets of Siena, watching Catherine Benincasa and wondering whether she may not have a word to say to us that may stop our pleasant vices. . . .[4]

So Jørgensen is a link in the chain of discovery of the historical St. Francis that began in the late nineteenth century, was like a beehive of activity through the 700th anniversary in 1926, and continued through at least the 1960s and 1970s. Without belaboring the point, I will offer one example of these links: the popular Greek writer Nikos Kazantzakis.

The internationally bestselling novelist of *Zorba the Greek* fame tells of reading Jørgensen's biography of St. Francis and being so inspired by it that he set out to find its author. Jørgensen, he'd heard, was living in Assisi. Their meeting took place near the end of Jørgensen's life when the Dane was an honorary citizen there and everyone knew him as the "white haired one."

For both Jørgensen and Kazantzakis, Francis's living presence in Assisi and the surrounding area birthed a sacred

4 John Howley, *Studies: An Irish Quarterly Review* 27, no. 108 (Dec. 1938): 672. The Latin means "acts of God accomplished through Catherine."

creativity and fueled a desire to serve God. Kazantzakis writes about this in several places. In Assisi with his wife he "wandered in shady lanes singing the *Fioretti*"! He was beginning then to write what would become his novel *God's Pauper* (published as *Saint Francis* in America). Kazantzakis found and befriended Jørgensen and wrote about the encounter in *Report to Greco*, his autobiography.[5] He recalls conversations they had while walking and talking. To those who love the spirit of St. Francis, these are all like riprap steps of apostolic succession—ones we might want to continue to trace as we approach the 800th anniversary of the death of Francis in 2026.

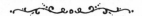

Part One of this book is the complete text of *Pilgrim Walks in Franciscan Italy*, a travel journal recounting experiences the biographer had while doing research for his biography of St. Francis. Jørgensen first visited Assisi in 1894 in the company of Mogens Ballin, a famous Danish painter and friend to Jørgensen, who was also a Jewish convert to Catholicism. The hilltop city of medieval mystery and mystical connotations grabbed hold of a young man questioning everything in his life at that time; Jørgensen would convert to Catholicism two years later. He would become a Franciscan tertiary three years after that.

5   Helen Kazantzakis, *Nikos Kazantzakis: A Biography Based on His Letters*, trans. P. A. Bien (New York: Bantam, 1966), 513 and 363–67.

As he writes in the opening chapter of *Pilgrim Walks*, it was nine years after that initial visit that he was touring Italy with a letter in his pocket from the General of the Order of Friars Minor. Father David Fleming, OFM, a member of the English province when appointed general on October 1, 1901, requested that all the superiors of houses in the Order afford Jørgensen hospitality. This worked.

The opening account—the visit to Greccio—took place in April 1903. Jørgensen explained later in his *Autobiography*:

> On April 21st I set out on this Franciscan pilgrimage of mine.
>
> It was not carried out without practical difficulties. My monetary means were small and my traveling equipment was limited to bare necessities: a bag slung over my shoulder, a cotton overcoat bought at Bocconoi's, a cheap umbrella, which was also to serve as a stick in the mountains, and not very many lira in my pocket.
>
> It was carried out with some anxiety. "Yesterday and today, unrest and fear because of my Franciscan studies. Am I wasting my time? Am I on the wrong track? Will I be able to support my family this way? Would it be better to give up the whole thing?" says my diary from a few weeks earlier (April 7).[6]

---

6   *An Autobiography,* trans. Ingeborg Lund, vol. 2 (London: Sheed & Ward, 1929), 254. See "Editor's Notes," below, for a summary of how I've altered the previously published translations of Jørgensen's work for this volume.

The whole pilgrimage lasted from April 21 to May 5, 1903.

In the preface to his Francis biography, Jørgensen notes how he put the finishing touches on that book in August 1906, a little more than three years later. The biography was published in 1907, quickly translated into many languages, appearing in English in 1912. Then he wrote a biography of Italy's other greatest saint, Catherine of Siena. Then in 1915 he moved to Assisi and spent most of the last forty-one years of his life there. The author of *Franciscan Poets* describes Jørgensen as "a Franciscan to his fingertips, a poet in every fiber of his being."[7] During World War II, he left briefly for Sweden, writing a biography of St. Bridget of Sweden there, only to return to Assisi when that massive work was completed. Jørgensen finally retired to his native Denmark in 1952 and died four years later at the age of eighty-nine. He is buried in Svendborg.

To this day, an Assisan street is named for Jørgensen. A plaque reads:

Via

Giovanni Joergensen

Poeta e Scrittore Danese

Cittadino Onorario d'Assisi

1866–1956

Già Via S. Maria delle Rose[8]

---

7 Benjamin Francis Musser, *Franciscan Poets* (New York: Macmillan, 1933), 142.

8 Giovanni Joergensen Street / Danish Poet and Writer / Honorary Citizen of Assisi / 1866–1956 / Formerly Via S. Maria delle Rose. (*Giovanni* is Italian for Johannes.)

In Part Two, you will find short writings from other books that help to illuminate *Pilgrim Walks*. Plus, there are interesting selections from Jørgensen's *Autobiography* from his pre-Catholic experiences in Assisi, a personal encounter he had with real *Béguines* in Bruges, and reflections on his relationship with another famous Catholic writer of the period, Léon Bloy.

It isn't my intention to make Johannes Jørgensen out to be a saint. He had his faults. For example, like many Catholics of his day he was too anxious to support political leaders and movements that would be likely to protect the recently obtained security of Catholics and Catholic institutions in European countries. For this reason, Jørgensen championed Benito Mussolini as one capable of defending the West, and the Church, from the growing spread of atheist Communism. It was only when the anti-clerical initiatives began in Italy that Jørgensen's support for the fascist waned.

He also left his wife and children in 1913, after many years of difficulties. Every marriage is complicated, and theirs was no exception. He doesn't write about this break, but he admits that for many years his poetic, romantic, itinerant life was a kind of infidelity to her.[9] As a Catholic, Jørgensen could not then remarry while his wife was still living. After she died in 1935, Jørgensen married again, two years later.

9   See Jørgensen, *An Autobiography,* vol. 2, 115, 156, etc.

But despite such realities, Jørgensen appeals to me for reasons beyond the admiration I have for his books. He was an early apostle of modern Franciscan studies, inheriting from Paul Sabatier a passion for research, uncovering the original spirit of Francis that had been lost, firsthand experience of Franciscan settings, and telling the story of a saint for pilgrims seeking answers to basic, universal doubts and questions. He was himself such a pilgrim, and his books about St. Francis communicate the seeking, questioning, and search for meaning of Francis's own life.

Pilgrim Walks is also a spiritual memoir of the first order—not only because of the author's talent for description, but because of the depth of his sharing of personal weaknesses. You will find him, for example, struggling with his own dark nights in ways that are similar to those of saints, in the chapter written at La Verna:

> While I lay there in the intense loneliness and silence, not hearing even the patter of rain outside, an appalling dread took over—a dread worse than that of death—the most awful fear that can weigh an unhappy mortal to the ground: the fear that he might, after all, not be the friend of God.

Jørgensen is also important to me for a more personal reason: It was Francis of Assisi who lured Jørgensen into the Catholic Church. This happened to me, too, about a century later, and also, I believe, through the intercession of St. Francis in my life. Jørgensen writes of his own lifelong conversion (to borrow a phrase from Thomas of Celano) beautifully in the two volumes of *An Autobiography*. He chronicles his life as a young intellectual and journalist, a poet and egotist, surfing in the ideas and cafés of the day, until he became, finally, obedient. This is the sense of his conversion. At one point, he describes it this way: "Not a refined 'spiritual' Christianity, but a humble stepping into the Church, hat in hand, like a peasant going into a cathedral."[10] I like that. Jørgensen was received into the Roman Catholic Church on February 16, 1896. Three years later, together with his wife, he became a Franciscan tertiary; that autumn, he was back in Assisi; and in December 1902, he began work on his biography of Francis.[11]

---

10 *An Autobiography*, vol. 1, 169. He is describing Mogens Ballin's conversion, here, but also foretelling his own.
11 *An Autobiography*, vol. 2, 108, 238.

PART
ONE

PILGRIM
WALKS
IN FRANCISCAN ITALY

CHAPTER 1
Greccio

URING THE WINTER OF 1904 I HAD FREQUENTLY looked northward with a pilgrim's yearning to the Galilee of St. Francis—Umbria, Tuscany, and the March of Ancona, the fairest region of fair Italy, hallowed by the footsteps of the saint, rich in historical and legendary lore. In my imagination I entered the ravines of the Apennines, the solitudes of the mountain forests, where the ancient hermitages are, the secluded monasteries dating from the earliest years of the Franciscan Order. I longed to visit these and other monasteries beyond the hills, of time immemorial, where everything is just the same today as it was in days gone by—to find myself within the very precincts of the venerable cloisters about which such wondrous stories are told.

Finally, one fine day in April, I was able to fulfill my wish and start my travels, with my primary destination being the valley of Rieti. In the same compartment with me was a priest with whom I entered into conversation. Naturally, we spoke of St. Francis, and of the great interest now generally taken in him and all that is closely associated with him. As the train wound its slow way up through the wild, mountainous region, my fellow traveler directed my attention to the principal points of interest: the picturesque old towns on the hillsides, whose towers and belfries stood out dark against the clear sky, and the gray feudal fortresses crowning the loftier heights.

Soon we emerged into a wide plain between vineyards, where verdant vine branches hang like garlands from tree to tree. In the far distance, above the purple hills, the crests of the snow-clad mountains were discernible, glistening in the sunshine. Then the train stopped. We were in Greccio, and cool mountain air greeted us as we emerged from the small station onto the main road.

Greccio consists of three distinct parts: the newest, close to the railway station; the old town high on the hillside; and the ancient Franciscan monastery, San Francesco di Greccio. The town, whose windows show dark on the gray walls of the houses, amid which rises a single bell tower, is on the left side of a sufficiently wide valley that extends for a considerable distance between the mountains. The monastery is on the right side of the valley, behind a thick forest of oaks and laurels.

Some accounts of this remarkable foundation were given to me by the priest while we walked together. But soon our roads parted. He went on to the town—he was attached to the church of Greccio—while I had to follow a stony path cut in the rock, which would bring me, in a little less than an hour, to the cloister on the height. "They have accommodation for strangers up there," were the last words my new friend said to me. So it was my good fortune that Greccio did not boast a single inn.

Then I went on my way alone. On my right rose the mountain, the blue-gray stone cropping up continually through the scanty grass, Alpen violets blossoming on the slope. On my left was the cultivated campaign, where young corn, already in the blade, formed a green carpet below the climbing vines. Perfect quiet prevailed all around—the sort of quiet that can only be found in the open country.

But listen! A soft sound breaks the stillness. Someone is singing in the distance. The voice is that of a child. The song I recognize at once as one of those strangely plaintive, lingering melodies I've often heard Umbrian peasants sing while working in the fields. I cannot quite make out the words, but about the tune there can be no mistake. Many times I've heard it wafted from the olive groves in the vicinity of Assisi on a tranquil autumn evening, when the mist is beginning to rise in the broad meadows. And later on, while the shades of night are falling, a solitary peasant girl, going home at the close of the day, is also heard singing in slow, measured cadence, that same sad sweet melody.

I sat down by the roadside to rest and the past rose vividly before me. Everything around me powerfully brought to mind that time when, having been admitted to the true Fold after long wanderings,[12] I spent a happy summer in the mountain seclusion of La Rocca, under Padre Felice's roof.[13] I noticed in the air the peculiar aromatic scent that is often experienced in Italian farm yards—the odor of withered maize leaves

12 He is referring ("true Fold") to his conversion—when he was welcomed into the Roman Catholic Church.
13 In 1894 he was in Assisi and other places important to St. Francis's living presence, close to converting to Catholicism. Jørgensen tells of these experiences in *An Autobiography,* vol. 1 (London: Sheed & Ward, 1948): "During the three months I spent at Assisi and La Rocca with Mogens Ballin (August, September, October) an unremitting warfare was being carried on within me." (267)

scattered about a threshing floor, and juniper branches emitting a pungent fragrance as they burn on a hearth. It told me that I could not be far from some human habitation. Then, on the hillside, beneath some straggling oaks, I saw several children picking up sticks. Approaching them, I asked a little girl with fair hair and blue eyes the way to the monastery. To answer, she turned around and, pointing to the rise above, said, "There it is!" There, in fact, it was, small and white, clinging to the rock, overshadowed by laurels and oaks. It was still a good way off, but the little girl showed me a shortcut through the convent vineyard and garden.[14] I clambered over a hedge and got into the garden.

It is a large enclosure, laid out in terraces on the slope of the mountain, full of tall trees, high grass, and wildflowers, blue hyacinths, and scarlet anemones. Occasionally, one comes upon a cultivated portion, sometimes planted with vines, or a loggia where lilies in pots are arranged in rows on the edge of the terrace.

I mounted terrace after terrace, always ascending, yet meeting no one. And the convent still stood high overhead, apparently as inaccessible, unapproachable as ever.

Then I heard someone call, and from behind some bushes stepped a sturdy, thick-set figure with features bronzed by the sun, curly hair, and bright brown eyes. It was a Franciscan. His brown habit was tied round his waist by a thick cord; his feet were bare; and in his hand he held a spade, which he rested on the ground while he stared in amazement at the stranger who

14 In English, "convent" is generally used only for houses of women and "monastery" for houses of men, but these two terms are interchangeable in Italian.

had intruded onto the convent grounds. Meanwhile, I hurried to produce the document with which the General of the Order of Friars Minor, Father David Fleming, had furnished me, commending me in most eulogistic terms to the Superiors of the Order, and expressing his wish that "the bearer should everywhere be made acquainted with the sacred traditions, and every facility should be afforded him for obtaining information respecting our holy Father Francis." No sooner did the bare-footed brother see the armorial bearings of the Order (the two arms crossed) at the head of the paper, and read the opening words, "Fr. David Fleming, *vicarius generalis totius ordinis patrum minorum*,"[15] than he bowed deferentially, stuck his spade in the earth, turned around and shouted: "Giuseppe! Giuseppe!"

At his call, Giuseppe, a much younger brother, but of the same scruffy sort, came forth. His habit was more soil-stained and even torn, and his bare feet were caked with mud that the sun had dried on them.

"Giuseppe, show this gentleman the way up to the monastery."

Accordingly, the young friar ran before me to a door in the garden wall, a door that opened onto a long flight of stone steps, which was the proper way up to the monastery. He closed the door behind me, and I began the ascent alone.

It was a very steep ascent. The steps were zigzagged and paved with small uneven stones. On one side was the declivity of the mountainside, clothed with rich vegetation of elegant ferns and dark laurels. On the other was a breastwork of chalk

15 "Fr. David Fleming, vicar general of the whole of the Order of the Friars Minor"

stones commanding an extensive view of the country. As I went on ascending the view became more and more wondrously beautiful. I leaned over the wall, and already the garden in which I'd been with the two Franciscans at work among the vines was dwarfed by distance. Soon, the steps emerged onto a terrace, from which I could see the whole valley of Rieti spread out below in panorama, partitioned into wide fields, some green, some brown, shut in by the mountaintops. The highest of these was snow-capped and half-shrouded by gray clouds.

In front of me was the entrance to the monastery, whose white walls really seemed to adhere to the rock and be suspended from it; it seemed the building was about to be detached and fall into the abyss. The gate was of the simplest kind. A door painted red, with a broken iron latch, led into a small outer room with a brick floor. A low, narrow window let in a little light, and then I saw another door that opened—or, stood open—onto a narrow passage constructed of planks that seemed to merge with whitewashed walls. A verse from the book of Tobit 4:23 was inscribed over this second door: "Fear not, my son: we lead indeed a poor life, but we shall have many good things." To the right of the door was a fresco painting of St. Francis; on the left, one of St. Anthony—both in gray habits. Under the representation of St. Anthony was a stone holy water stoup with the date MDLXII.[16] Close by, a latticed gate led into a chapel, over which were the words: "In this chapel, dedicated to St. Luke, Francis prepared a resting place for Christ in the crib."

16 1562.

There, then, exactly at the entrance of the cloister, was the spot where Christmas night was celebrated in Greccio. I gazed through the lattice, but it was all dark within. After a short pause I proceeded on my way down the long corridor, the boards of which were in many places very loose. A bell wire ran the whole length along the ceiling.

I then turned a corner. Over an archway there was a wooden shield with the Franciscan arms. Underneath it was the word *Silentium*. I went through into a kind of entrance hall, or vestibule, floored with wood, which is not usual in Italy, and which Francis desired for love of poverty. On one side, shut off by another wooden lattice, was a small chapel with two windows looking out over the valley. On the other, a rickety staircase leading to the upper story of the monastery. The naked rock formed the background. Fronting me was a closed door that appeared to shut off the continuation of the corridor along which I had come, and beside it was an open passage beyond which all was pitch darkness.

Not knowing what was before me there, I preferred to ascend the staircase. It was narrow, and so low that I had to stoop to avoid striking my head against the worm-eaten beams. I imagined I heard someone overhead, and stood still to listen, but it was only the slow, monotonous ticking of a large clock nearby. Going in the direction of the sound, I came to a narrow corridor between two rows of small rooms painted brown. These were the cells; the doors were without locks, but a cord passing through a hole in each door afforded the means of lifting the latch that was inside. My footsteps sounded noisy in the stillness. I knocked on one after another of the low doors, but no one answered.

I wandered about in this strange labyrinth of poverty and brown paint, up and down flights of stairs, through rooms so dark that I had to grope my way about in them, then out onto little balconies in great need of repair, looking down upon the valley. At last, at the very top, I reached a kind of gallery constructed against the face of the live rock, where big piles of laurel branches were stacked and golden broom and purple juniper blossomed in the crevices of the blue-gray stone. I could go no farther: a closed door at the end of the gallery, leading into the forest, forbade further progress.

So back I went, past other odd nooks and corners, past the noisily ticking clock, finally stumbling into a small, narrow, dimly lit church with wooden candlesticks on the altar and old choir stalls blackened and shiny from long centuries of use. Through a low door I emerged then into the open air, onto a tolerably large platform flagged with tiles. A few steps lower down was the very door by which a short time earlier I had entered the monastery. So I had been all over it and found no one at home. Disappointed and—why should I not own it?—a little hungry, I seated myself on the doorstep. A good time and place, I thought, to read the eighth chapter of the *Fioretti*—the chapter about "Perfect Joy."[17]

17 *Fioretti*, "Little Flowers," shorthand for *The Little Flowers of St. Francis*, a fourteenth-century collection of legends of the saint. Jørgensen translated the *Fioretti* into Danish. The chapter "Perfect Joy" may be found in two of my other books: *Francis of Assisi in His Own Words: The Essential Writings*, 2nd Edition (2018) and *Lord, Make Me an Instrument of Your Peace* (2020).

There I sat for a long time. Five o'clock came, half-past five, ten minutes to six: there was not a sound in the deserted monastery, only the wind rushing through the corridors made the doors creak. Eventually, far down below, the two friars who I saw in the garden made their appearance. Their day's work was done. They came up the flight of steps, arms full of vegetables for supper. I pocketed the *Fioretti*, and a few minutes later I was seated in the refectory with a piece of bread and a glass of wine, which the older of the two gardeners, who was also the cook, set before me.

There I sat while Brother Humilitas—for that was the cook's name—chatted pleasantly with me; and there I was when the Father Guardian came in from the forest, where, according to the good Franciscan custom, he had spent part of the day, not with a book of poetry, but with a volume of the works of St. Leonard of Port Maurice, *The Treasure Hidden beneath the Veil of the Holy Eucharist.*[18]

The Guardian laid his book down on the table while he examined my letters of recommendation. His physiognomy reminded me of a golden eaglet: his eye was bright; his glance keen; his complexion dark; and his hair black as ebony. Very carefully and attentively he perused the Latin sentences written by his General. Then he suddenly looked up, turned

18 Italian Franciscan preacher, missionary, and ascetic writer (1676–1751). The book Jørgensen spied in the guardian's hand was first published in English in Dublin: *The Hidden Treasure: Or the Immense Excellence of the Holy Sacrifice of the Mass* (James Duffy, 1861). Here's a summary from the opening paragraph: "Have you considered what the holy sacrifice of the Mass really is? It is the sun of Christianity, the soul of Faith, the centre of the Catholic religion, the grand object of all her rites, ceremonies, and Sacraments; in a word, it is the condensation of all that is good and beautiful in the Church of God."

sharply toward me, and pointing to my glass said with an air of command, "*Beva!*" (Drink your wine!)

After I had complied with this injunction, and agreed to a second glass, the Father Guardian led the way to his cell. It was one of the little rooms with a door upon which I had earlier knocked in vain. It was almost incredibly small, and lighted from above. The furniture consisted of nothing but a table, some bookshelves, and a few rush-bottom chairs.

While we were talking, the light faded quickly, and soon the evening bell rang. Father Guardian stood up. "We always go into the church at this time," he said. In the corridor outside it was pitch-dark, so that I ran up against some of the friars who were going by. Then I felt a guiding hand take mine, and, stooping our heads, we passed through a low doorway. By the dim light of a single oil lamp, I recognized the church where I had found myself earlier in the afternoon. With a wave of the hand, the Father Guardian showed me where to kneel, and the night prayers began.

Father Guardian knelt beside me. As my eyes gradually grew accustomed to the half-light, I glimpsed two, three, then more figures in the stalls. On the bare floor just in front of me was a ragged brother kneeling with arms outstretched and palms turned upward. I glanced stealthily at the others and saw that several had theirs extended in a similar manner. Later on, when I was at Mount La Verna, I learned why this attitude in prayer is peculiar to the Franciscan Order.

The profound silence was broken by the Father Guardian's voice beginning the prayers, all of which were in Latin.

"*Santus, sanctus, sanctus Dominus Deus noster omnipotens, qui est, et qui erat, et qui venturus est.*"—"Holy, holy, holy Lord God Almighty, who was, and who is, and who is to come."

And the friars responded: "*Et laudemus et superexaltemus eum in saecula.*"—"Let us praise and magnify Him forever."

Father Guardian: "You are worthy, O Lord our God, to receive glory and honor and power and benediction."

The brothers: "Let us praise and magnify Him forever."

"Worthy is the Lamb that was slain to receive power and divinity and wisdom and strength and honor and glory and benediction."

The others responded as before, and for some time they continued this antiphonal chant, which was encouraged by St. Francis. It ended with the usual doxology. Then followed the prayers—first the beautiful prayer that St. Francis wrote two years before his death:

Almighty, most holy, most high God, the supreme and only Good, to you we give all praise and honor and glory. We bless you and give thanks to you for all you have given to us. You are the God of gods, who alone does wonders. You are the triune, the one only God, the Lord of lords, the living and true God. You are our hope, our justice, all our riches. You are our protector, our defender, our guardian, our refuge, and our strength. You are infinite goodness, the great and marvelous Lord God, almighty, gracious, merciful, and our Redeemer.

Almighty, eternal, just, and merciful God, grant that
we, your poor servants, may always do what we know
to be your will, and always will what is pleasing in your
sight, so that, purified and enlightened and kindled by
the fire of your Holy Spirit, we may follow in the foot-
prints of your beloved Son, Jesus Christ our Lord, and
by your grace may finally behold you in that blessed
country where you, O Most High, live and reign and are
adored, God Almighty, forever and ever. Amen.

That is the evening oblation that Francis taught to his disciples. After it came the long rosary in honor of the Seven Joys
of Our Lady. A short pause ensued, then I heard the rattle of
matches in a box. A lantern was lit, and in the bright flame
all that I had seen before only dimly stood out now in relief
against the darkness. By the light of the lantern one of the
fathers read a portion of a spiritual book in the monotonous,
level tone prescribed by monastic rule for such readings. The
subject was the necessity of meditation on the four last things:
death, judgment, heaven, and hell. Then the light was extinguished and mental prayer followed.

I think I may say that in the course of my life I have met
with much that was uncommon and affecting, yet scarcely
ever with anything that impressed me so profoundly as those
minutes of perfect silence among the Franciscans of Greccio.
As I knelt amid those barefooted, brown-habited friars, who
in the darkness raised their hands and their hearts to heaven
in voiceless prayer, I realized more vividly than ever before
what the Middle Ages were—how far removed the twentieth

century was—how far away beyond the crest of the mountains was the modern world, and how remote the great, busy towns, with their glare and noise, unrest and endless amusements, seemed. Nothing seemed real to me, then, except that humble little chapel of the poor, primitive monastery where the sons of St. Francis prayed, gave thanks, and offered praise to God— the God to whom the admirers of the world gave hardly a passing thought.

How long this profound silence, this absorption in prayer, lasted I am not sure. Occasionally, someone made a slight movement or sighed. Then footsteps were heard: one of the brothers rose and left the choir. Shortly after, the monastery bell rang, echoing out over the tranquil valley for the last time that evening. It rang what in ancient times was the curfew bell: the signal that all lights were to be extinguished and fires covered until the next morning.

As the last stroke of the bell died away, a hand took mine as before. Soon we were all assembled in the refectory, where the flame of a common, unshaded gas lamp seemed to pierce the eyes. Before we sat down to table, the Father Guardian introduced me to the two young fathers who I had seen in the choir.

After supper, there were a few prayers in the chapel, then away we went to the common room where there was a fire. Although it was April, the weather was very cold, and in Greccio it was necessary to warm oneself before going to bed. So we all gathered in a semicircle—some sitting, some standing—around the large, open fireplace, while Friar Giuseppe piled large logs on the andirons.

"That young man is clever at lighting fires," said Brother Humilitas, approvingly.[19]

Colored with pleasure and exertion, Friar Giuseppe then struck a lucifer match—one of the old-fashioned ones, smelling of brimstone, that were in use a half-century ago—and soon a great fire of laurel branches flared and blazed under the logs.[20] Our shadows, of gigantic size, danced on the walls and ceiling in the fitful firelight.

At the end of the row of friars stood the Father Guardian, staring with eagle gaze into the fire and holding out his hands to get them thoroughly warm. Beside me on the narrow bench sat Friar Secondo, gentle, quiet, and serene—accustomed, as his name implies, never to be first, but always to sit modestly in a corner.[21] However, you only need to begin to talk with him and soon you perceive that few are so well-acquainted with the life of St. Francis, or so conversant with the history of the Franciscan Order, as old Friar Secondo.

"Here we sit," I said to him, "enjoying the company of Brother Fire, who is beauteous and merry and mighty and strong, and who illumines the night."[22]

"Yes," he answered, and his eyes smiled under his shaggy, white eyebrows. "Brother Fire was the element that our Father Francis loved best of all. In fact, our father treated fire so

19 In the acknowledgments of his biography of Francis, Jørgensen thanks "Brother Humilitas of Assisi."
20 These were matches once branded "Lucifer," which were self-igniting: they could be lit by striking on any surface.
21 In Italian, *Secondo* means simply "Second"; but if, as Jesus said, "So shall the last be first, and the first last" (Matt. 20:16), then a humble friar might choose the name *Secondo*.
22 Jørgensen is quoting from Francis's "Canticle of the Creatures."

34

tenderly that he would not permit the brothers to throw a burning wick on the ground, as one often does, to stamp it out. He would always have them lay it down reverently, because fire is our brother, created by the same God who created us."

"We are not so pious," Father Chrysostom observed, as he flicked a spark off his sleeve.

"No," said Father Silverio, with a smile. "But then, fire doesn't have the same respect for us that it had for St. Francis. You know what happened when he was living over there in Fonte Colombo—which you (he said, turning to me) will no doubt visit in the course of your pilgrimage. His eyes were, by then, very weak, from all the tears he had shed for his sins. He could hardly see. Brother Elias, who was general of the order, and Cardinal Ugolino, got one of the physicians attached to the papal court to visit St. Francis. After examining his eyes, the physician said he must apply a red-hot iron above the eye that was more seriously affected. So they brought a brazier filled with hot coals. The doctor's assistant stood by with a bellows to blow on the fire, and soon the instrument was as red as a cherry.

"But before the operation took place, St. Francis went up to the fire and addressed it, saying, 'Brother Fire, you are more noble and more useful than most created things. I have always been fond of you, and I always will be, for love of God who created you. Now, show yourself gentle and kind toward me, and don't burn me more severely than I can bear.' And he made the sign of the cross over the red-hot iron. Then the physician applied the iron, and the brothers fled in horror.

Francis himself, however, didn't speak a single word or utter a cry. And when the operation was over, he said to the physician: 'If it isn't sufficiently burned, sear it again, for I didn't feel any pain.'"

That was Father Silverio's tale. The Father Guardian said nothing; he only smiled as he stood there holding out his hands to the fire. But it was time for our séance to break up. Friar Giuseppe began to rake together the hot coals for a warming pan, which, as it turned out, was destined for my bed. With many reciprocal good wishes, we parted.

Soon I was alone in the guest chamber, the best cell in the monastery. It is large enough to fit a good-sized bed, a *prie-dieu*, a small iron washstand, and a modest set of earthenware. In the whitewashed walls were two cupboards—the larger one a wardrobe, and the other, a place to stow my small amount of luggage. The cell itself was not more than five feet in length and the same in width.

I opened the window—the shutters were on the inside— and leaned out a narrow aperture that was hardly more than a loophole.[23] Across from me were the mountains. The stretched-out plain was below. There were a few stars in the sky. I heard the sound of the stream in the valley, and the distant croaking of frogs.

Leaving the window open, I came back inside within the four walls of the room, which was lighted by a tall candle in

23 "Loophole" is an old term for a feature of medieval architecture: a narrow slit/window in an outside wall, through which arrows could be fired on attackers.

a brass candlestick on the *prie-dieu*. A picture hung over the bed. A crucifix was over the *prie-dieu*. Beside the door there was a holy water font. Otherwise, the walls were bare. Yet in this simple chamber I felt happy and comfortable, as I have seldom felt in any other place in the wide world.

I took out my watch to wind it, and found the hands pointing only to nine-thirty. I put it down on the *prie-dieu* at the head of the bed, and proceeded to leisurely undress, with that feeling of content that one might have returning to the home of one's childhood after a long absence, inhabiting again the room where one slept as a boy. I left the window open and put out the light. And in my dreams mingled the noise of the brook rushing down the hillside and the croaking of the frogs in the distant meadows.

CHAPTER 2

A Day
in the Monastery

I WAS AWAKE THE NEXT MORNING AT A LITTLE BEFORE six o'clock. There was a knock at the door, and a voice said, "*È tempo di Messa!*" ("Mass time!") I heard the birds twittering outside the window, and looking at my bed, saw that the counterpane was covered with cotton of a yellow, flowery pattern—what excessive elegance! The room itself was floored with flagstones, not with boards like the rest of the monastery.

I began to get dressed, but in a few moments the cook, the one who had woken me, came back and said: "Signor Giovanni, the Mass is beginning." I hurriedly thrust my arms into my coat and rushed to the door, which Brother Humilitas pointed out to me. I found that my room was very near the church, something I didn't notice the evening before. I only had to go through the little library. Close to the library door was the entrance to the church—to that section of it, at least, that was in front of the altar. The choir, where prayers were said the previous evening, was behind it.

I entered. Father Silverio was standing before the altar. Brother Secondo was kneeling in one of the ancient stalls. Behind the choir screen, some of the colorful handkerchiefs that Italian peasant women often wear on their heads were dimly discernible in the half-light. After the priest's Communion, two of the peasant girls came forward to receive

Holy Communion. They remained kneeling for a long time on the lowest step of the altar, motionless in an attitude of recollection and devotion. Not a shadow of change passed over their strongly marked, regular features.

When I returned to my room, I opened the window that Brother Humilitas had shut when he came to tidy the apartment. The wind blew in cold; the sky was overcast; heavy clouds hung over the lofty mountain, whose gray flanks were planted with olive trees and vines, still leafless. The town of Greccio was far in the distance on the other side of the valley. I could see three brown-clad figures walking along the road in that direction. They were three friars on their way to the village, where someone had died during the night.

In the refectory, a cup of black coffee was served to me, with some slices of toast. Brother Humilitas, who was waiting on me, hurried in such a way that he accidentally let the bread fall to the ground. Putting it away, he kissed it, as if to ask its forgiveness. Later on, I noticed that before every meal the young novices always kissed the piece of bread that was placed under their napkin. This reverence for our daily bread, indeed for everything that pertains to our earthly existence or promotes life, is truly Franciscan. The spirit of the Order is essentially one of reverence. The veneration and love due to God are extended to all his creatures for his sake.

I soon left the refectory and retired to the library, next to my cell. There, on simple shelves behind wire netting were hundreds of volumes, both Latin and Italian, bound in parchment. I took down several of them, including a small, beautifully printed collection of St. Bonaventure's lesser known writings. I opened at random and read an edifying description of "The Different Grades and Works of Humility."

After replacing the little book on the shelf, I went to the window again. Clouds had come down on the gray mountains and would soon hide the town of Greccio from view. The country looked bare and deserted. No one was to be seen except a solitary peasant down in the valley, walking slowly under a huge green umbrella. There was dense fog. Not a sound could be heard except the heavy downpour of rain. I was a prisoner in my monastic solitude.

I looked at my watch. It was only nine-thirty. It was cold in my room, so I put on my overcoat and began to walk up and down. But there wasn't room to move about in the narrow apartment, so finally, with ice-cold feet and numb fingers I sat in front of the small, rickety writing table in the library. Before me various books and pamphlets were sitting, and among them was one that excited my interest: a work by Father Benedetto Spila titled *The Reformed Franciscan Monasteries in the Roman Province*.[24]

Reform in the Franciscan Order is of discipline, not doctrine. Each century has witnessed such reforms, necessitated by the constant propensity of fallen humanity to fix a lower standard for themselves. Even during the lifetime of St. Francis there were some of his younger disciples who wanted the austerity

24 Benedetto Spila, OFM, was a priest, and then bishop, who authored several books. He died in 1928.

of the Rule to be relaxed, particularly when it came to the strict evangelical poverty that the saint required his followers to observe. After his death, the Order divided into two camps: the Conventuals, or relaxed; and the Spirituals, or friars of the strict observance. These latter rallied around the senior friars—the *compagni* of the saint—and most of all around Brother Leo, the confessor, secretary, confidant, and intimate friend of Francis, the living fount of pure and genuine Franciscan traditions. And to them, at their request, were handed over the oldest and poorest houses of the Order—*loca paupercula, nec minus devota*—poor little places, but in their poverty no less sacred. Life at Greccio is restricted to the simplest wants. There is little to mark the days as they pass: prayer, work, the refreshment of the body that is absolutely necessary, and that is all, beyond the pure, quiet happiness of living together in brotherly love. Or, as an old Franciscan writer expressed it, "through Francis to be one in Christ."

Several hours passed quickly while I was studying Father Spila's book. One has an abundance of time for work in a religious house: first, the long morning, from eight o'clock, when one has had coffee, until a quarter to twelve, when the bell rings for prayers in choir, and afterwards for the midday meal; then the whole afternoon, until the Angelus rings at about seven-fifteen, when everyone assembles for prayers in the church. Then there is, after supper, and recreation in the common room, still time that can be made use of before going to bed. No wonder then that voluminous works, such as those of the Benedictine monks, or the *Annals of the Friars Minor*, have been compiled in the cloister.[25]

After dinner, I lay down to sleep for a while. A siesta forms part of the daily routine of a well-ordered monastery. Also, the weather was still inclement and rough; the wind had picked up and was driving the rain in sheets across the deserted plain. Towering above the cultivated mountainsides, clothed with verdant fields, still leafless oaks, and poplars in their fresh young green, the naked mountain ridge rose bleak and gray, washed clean by the heavy rain and furrowed by many rivulets.

When I woke from my midday slumber, I found that the rain had stopped. It had made a vast lake of the meadows in the valley. There were now gleams of bright sunshine, which gilded the distant towers of Rieti and illumined the reddish-brown hills that shut in the valley on the south. I left my room and went to the chapel, where I found Brother Secondo on his knees, with a cat resting at his feet. The cat purred contentedly, while Friar Secondo occasionally whispered a word to her.

I slipped out again, noiselessly, and stepped onto the terrace before the chapel. Going down a few steps I came to the little chapel erected on the spot where the Crib once stood. It was so dark inside that at first I could see nothing, but when my eyes became accustomed to the darkness, I perceived that I was in a small, vaulted room, and that facing the door, close to it, was an altar, above which was a Madonna

25 *Annales Minorum* is the monumental work of Irish Franciscan and historian Father Luke Wadding, OFM (1588–1657), published in eight volumes over a twenty-nine-year period.

of fourteenth-century origin, with the Divine Child and St. Joseph. To the left, in the darkest corner of all, was a highly interesting fresco representing the Christmas night in Greccio when, at St. Francis's desire, our Lord's Nativity was solemnly celebrated in the forest in as realistic a manner as possible, in the presence of a large crowd of devout worshipers. I examined the fresco closely by the light of a candle and was charmed by the countenance of the saint: the happy smile. The almost lamb-like expression resting on it agrees well with what Thomas of Celano says in the familiar legend.[26]

Another work of art, even more remarkable than the fresco, is preserved in the monastery of Greccio. It is a portrait of St. Francis painted during his lifetime, at the direction of the Lady Jacoba dei Settesoli. The Father Guardian took me to see it. It is placed above the altar of a small chapel opening out of the entrance hall of the monastery and concealed by a curtain. The figure of the saint is short and slight, the countenance emaciated and worn. All the stigmata are plainly marked, except on the left hand, which holds a handkerchief to the face. In this same chapel are preserved a few relics of St. Francis. A small devotional picture, which he was in the habit of carrying about with him, is interesting as it testifies to his love for the Christmas festival; it is an enamel painting of the Blessed Virgin and St. Joseph adoring the newborn infant Jesus. Beside it stands a small, extremely simple brass crucifix, and two equally unpretentious brass candlesticks that were

26 Thomas of Celano—friar, historian, poet, and friend of St. Francis—was Francis's first biographer. Jørgensen is reflecting here on one of the sources for his own biography of the saint.

used whenever Brother Leo, or any other priest of the order, said Mass for Brother Francis.

While visiting the curiosities of the monastery, Father Guardian took me to the cell formerly inhabited by the saint—a room now completely dark, since a wall was built before it. Originally, it was a cavern in the rock. To give me a better idea of what the cell was like, my guide led me up above the convent, through a narrow path that ran along the face of the rock. There he opened a trapdoor in the ground, gathered his brown habit closely round him, and descended some rough steps hewn in the rock. I followed him, and we were soon standing in the cave where Blessed John of Parma shut himself up for thirty-two years to pray, fast, and do penance. It is a kind of gigantic, cup-like shell, formed by nature, set upright and built into the rock. It is not high enough for a man to stand in, and how anyone could contrive to sleep there is incomprehensible, as it would be impossible to stretch out in it. Seeing this grotto, I understood why Giotto always represents the disciples of St. Francis in such strange postures when sleeping—crouched down, their backs bent, their knees drawn up. Perhaps we can conclude that the artist, himself a Franciscan tertiary, visited these lowly hermitages and carefully observed the way of life of those brothers who kept up the traditions of the heroic age of the Order.

In front of the cell, on a projection of the rock, stands a tiny chapel, or rather, a short, narrow, open portico with an altar at one end and a stone bench at the other. Above it is a scanty roof resting on wooden pillars. From this spot, one has a magnificent and extensive view of the whole valley of Rieti. At the moment I saw it, the valley was wrapped in a light, warm haze of ethereal blue. There, at that altar, Father Pacifico told me that Blessed John of Parma used to say Mass daily. A lay brother used to come down to minister to him. One day when the brother failed to make his appearance an angel took his place and served the Mass.[27]

At my request, Father Pacifico left me alone in the tiny chapel. A bit of wall with a low door in it shuts it off from the grotto, into which I returned to gaze once more with amazement and almost horror at the bare, rugged rock that for thirty-two years formed the bed of the sainted friar. And when I emerged again into the light—that wondrous light in which the setting sun of Italy bathes mountain and valley—I tried to imagine the life led by Blessed John and many other solitaries from both earlier and later times.

That very morning, while it was raining, I had become concerned about my hands, thinking what a grievance it was to sit shut up in a small, unheated room to read hour after hour, shivering with cold. How would I have felt, being not in the sheltered cell of a convent, surrounded by books, but in an open grotto exposed to the rage of the elements, barefoot, clad in a tattered habit, my library consisting of only a breviary and a crucifix? Then, to live there not for just a few days or weeks, but year after year, for a lifetime! It is almost impossible for the ordinary Christian to imagine a life of such self-mortification, such extraordinary fervor.

27 Bl. John of Parma (1209–1289) was minister-general of the Order for ten years. In 1257, he retired to Greccio to live in solitude.

While we were sitting around the fire later that evening, Father Pacifico brought in a relic which I had heard was in his possession: the much talked-of iron for making hosts which St. Francis gave to the monastery of Greccio. It consists of two round plates of iron, resembling tongs, with a long handle on each side. It is considered a curiosity as well as a precious relic of the saint. It was passed from hand to hand as we sat there, and I closely examined the stamp on one of the two circular plates. The design on the upper surface of the altar breads is now usually either a crucifix, an Agnus Dei, or the monogram I.H.S. But none of these are on this thirteenth-century mold: only flourishes and some letters, which no one present seemed able to explain. As far as I could discern in the firelight, the letters appeared to be the first three letters of the name of Jesus in Greek—I.H.C.— the bar of the H having been omitted, it would seem, for the sake of the ornamental flourishes.

My time at Greccio was almost at an end. I had been there three days, and the following morning, I knew I had to move on.

The evening meal was finished, and we were in the chapel to give thanks. Before supper, I'd heard for the last time the cheery voices of the three fathers call to me across the table, after the friendly Franciscan custom: *"Buona sera, Signor Giovanni, e buon appetito!"*[28] And while in the chapel, I'd

28 "Good evening, Mr. Giovanni. Eat well!"

heard for the last time the curfew bell ring over the valley with the bell whose iron tongue was afterward silent until it rang again the following morning to call us to early Mass.

This was the last evening that Friar Giuseppe would shovel the glowing embers from the hearth for my warming-pan, and I imagined he conducted me to my room and brought me hot water more ceremoniously than before. Then he went away, and I opened my window as I had done on my first night at Greccio and leaned out. No stars were to be seen: all was shrouded in darkness. Only in the far distance could I discern a glimpse of the electric lights in Rieti.

On the following morning, I was awakened by the sound of the bell for first Mass. It was five-fifteen. I rose at once. It had rained during the night, but the clouds were clearing. The sun shone brightly over the verdant plain below and the birds were singing in the convent garden. Through the library, the door of which Friar Giuseppe must have left open the night before, the Father Guardian's voice reached my ear: "*Gloria in excelsis Deo!*" I hurried into the chapel.

After Mass, I said farewell to my little room, to the library, to the lovely view of the town of Rieti, and the undulating hills beyond, seen from its two small windows. Father Guardian came to the refectory to say goodbye, and I said goodbye to Brother Humilitas. I did not see the others. Then I went regretfully down by the same steps, on the same path up which I'd come only three days before—how could it have been so little time? On my way, I met peasants going up to hear Mass: boys and young men with handsome, innocent-looking faces, clear olive complexions, black eyes and hair, sturdy, well-mannered young men. I couldn't help thinking, I wish I was as good a man, as good a Catholic, as these simple sons of the soil.

Then I went down into the valley, past the spring where the women were washing linen three days ago. Again and again, I turned to look back at the monastery, at its olive-tinted walls, and the new part that is white. At last, as I got farther down the ravine, it disappeared behind the wood of oak and laurel. Out beyond in the wide plain the rain of the night before had left big expanses of water; their surface gleamed like burnished silver. The air began to feel warm. I had to pick up my pace to reach Rieti in time for the train. As I went on, I heard once more from afar the strangely solemn sound of the Greccio bells.

CHAPTER 3
Fonte Colombo

I N THE AFTERNOON, THE DAY ON WHICH MY VISIT TO
GRECCIO ended, I started on a fresh pilgrimage, my destination being the monastery of Monte, or Fonte Colombo.[29]
The mountain was originally known as Monte Rainerio, on
account of the many clear, cold springs that take their rise there.
But St. Francis, foreseeing that many of his sons would draw
water from those springs, called the place *Fons Columbarum*
(Fount of Doves), and the monastery he founded there bears
that name to this day.

It was two o'clock when I passed out of the Porta Romana,
in Rieti. At a short distance from the town I turned off to
the right, following a road that led me first along the foot of
high, barren, precipitous limestone rocks, then upward over
wooded heights where blue anemones and purple violets grew
in profusion between the tree trunks. I asked for directions
from several people and gradually made it higher up among
the mountains. Soon I left hamlets and fields behind me.

The way led over a barren space of pebbles and flint stones,
and over wide, rough, rugged places. Tiny rivulets, clear as
crystal, welled out of the ground. The narrow, stony path ran

29 Fonte Colombo is a Franciscan convent between Greccio and Rieti. In
the life of St. Francis, it is reverenced as the place where he wrote the
Rule of 1223, and where, two years later, he underwent eye surgery.

along the verge of a deep gorge, at the bottom of which a mountain stream swollen by rain was rushing noisily. On the other side of the gorge rose another mountain, clothed with forest. On its summit were buildings and a small bell tower. It was Fonte Colombo.

I walked on, following the path mechanically. The whole mountain overflowed now with clear, trickling streams. There was nothing to do but wade through them.

I paused a moment and looked back. From the crest that I'd reached, I could see, down below, smaller crags, a verdure-clad plain intersected by white roads, the gray towers of Rieti, and behind Rieti, the lofty Abruzzi partly shrouded in indigo-colored clouds partly glinting in sharply defined sunbeams. In the vast solitude, not a sound was to be heard except the gurgling of the stream at the foot of the descent.

The road descended all the way to that stream, and then ascended again on the other side. A flight of steps cut in the mountainside helped facilitate the last steep ascent, and after having walked continuously for two hours, I finally found myself standing before the convent on a wide green space hedged round with boxwood. In the center was a wooden cross painted red—the Franciscan cross, such as one always sees in front of the houses of the Gray Friars.[30]

I stood still for a few minutes to catch my breath and look around. To the left of the monastery I saw a closed gate that apparently goes to the rear of the building. Over it is a Latin

30 Gray Friars, or Grayfriars (or Greyfriars, in Britain), is a term used to mean the Order of Friars Minor, the First Order of Franciscans, founded by St. Francis.

inscription—the words that Yahweh spoke to Moses out of the burning bush: "Put off the shoes from thy feet: for the place whereon thou standest is holy ground." The impression made by the sight of these words was so forcible, so solemn, in the midst of this wild, desolate solitude, high up between the vast mountains, that I felt as if I must obey the command.

Those who have traveled in mountainous regions will understand me, for there is something about the grandeur of the mountains that impresses one with a sense of the majesty and greatness of God more than anything else in nature. No wonder that Francis of Assisi returned over and over to mountain solitudes, to have conversations with the Almighty.

I had ample leisure to make these reflections, because although I rang the monastery bell repeatedly, I couldn't get in. The brothers must have been taking their siesta. After a while, however, I heard the familiar sound of wooden sandals on the flagstones. I rang again—rang loudly. In a few minutes, I was seated in the refectory taking some refreshment that the vivacious, smiling, young Father Guardian Giovanni da Greccio offered me.

As soon as I had satisfied my hunger, the Father Guardian proposed that we should visit the Sanctuarium, the hallowed spot where Francis prayed, fasted, and wrote the Rule.[31] We walked through the door over which I'd seen the inscription. A narrow path led alongside the monastery walk, on which the Stations of the Cross were erected. On the side overlooking the descent, the path is protected by a low parapet.

31 *Sanctuarium* is Latin for Sanctuary. In Italian, it's *Santuario*.

We stopped first at a small Gothic chapel—the oratory dedicated in honor of the Blessed Virgin and mentioned in an old chronicle.[32] Within it are the remains of some fresco paintings. We then descended by some zigzagged steps to the hallowed spot itself. The steep rock hangs over the abyss. On a level with the tops of the trees—evergreen oaks, elms, and maples—that grow in the chasm below, are the entrances to two grottos. One was once inhabited by Brother Leo; the other by St. Francis. They reach into the interior of the rock.

A wooden balcony projecting over the abyss leads into St. Francis's hermitage. First comes a small chapel, with mountain rock on one side. A strong stone wall of rough masonry protects the narrow ledge of rock that constituted the saint's sleeping place. A trapdoor in the ground leads down to his oratory—his most private, secret chamber. It is simply a chasm in the rock, open at both ends, and so narrow that one touches both walls at every moment.

The farther end opens out onto the valley. The descent is abrupt and precipitous until the mountainside is lost to sight in the depths of the forest below. Almost involuntarily, one keeps still in this place, the solemnity of the solitude is so impressive. We stood there motionless for some time. Outside, the wind roared in the forest. One heard the river rushing below, and the splash of the falling rain—the same three voices that Francis heard during the nights and days he spent there in solitary prayer nearly seven hundred years ago.

32 An oratory is a small chapel, often for private worship.

We ascended again to the convent, and the Father Guardian locked the door through which we passed. Pointing to the words above it, he said with a smile: "Pope Sixtus IV obeyed that admonition literally. He was a Franciscan himself, so to go barefoot was no novelty to him."[33]

Our visit to the grottos in the rock took quite a long time. The afternoon sun, nearing the horizon, poured its golden light on the space before the house. Two white goats were feeding there. One of them went up to the Father Guardian, bleating gently, to be petted.

After night prayers and supper, I took my seat with the four fathers of the monastery for the usual hour of recreation. It seemed not to be the custom, as it was at Greccio, to assemble around the fire, but instead in the Father Guardian's cell. It was a good-sized room, and there was space for all of us. The monastery of Fonte Colombo is much larger in size than the one in Greccio, because it's one of the novitiates of the Order. I passed the evening in conversation with the fathers. When ten o'clock struck, I was alone in my room. It was a dark night; white, lusterless clouds hung over the mountains. Not a sound was heard but the gurgle of the stream in the ravine below.

I passed some of the following morning indoors, studying a vellum-bound book of Sabatier on the Poverello, the Poor

---

33 He's referring to the Latin inscription of words God spoke to Moses out of the burning bush: "Remove the shoes from your feet, for the place where you are standing is holy ground."

Man of Assisi. Then I went outdoors, under the fairest of skies, to enjoy the bright sunshine. I watched the shadows of clouds as they flitted over limestone rocks, deepening already dark shades of the woods on the mountainside—the only somber spots in the landscape. Far in the distance I could glimpse the belfry of the town of Greccio, and even farther away, the white walls of its solitary monastery. Meanwhile, I was sitting with my back against a huge block of moss-grown rock. Around me, forget-me-nots and anemones rose out of the moss and turf. On the summits of the mountains was the glitter of freshly fallen snow, yet where I was sitting the sun was almost hot.

In the afternoon, I again visited St. Francis's Grotto, in the company of all the men of the monastery. It was Saturday, and it is the custom at Fonte Colombo on that day, shortly before sunset, to commemorate the passing away of St. Francis. In remembrance of his last hour, all of us—old and young, fathers and novices, lay brothers and me, a stranger—went from the church to the little chapel over St. Francis's rocky cell. Two-by-two the long line of brown-habited figures filed along the path beside the monastery wall, and then descended the long flight of steps. The Father Guardian was right in front of me. With his clear, powerful voice he led the singing, which was taken up by the strong young voices. The melody was a peculiar one—at the same time mournful and jubilant. The Latin words were very simple.

Eventually, we reached the sanctuary. It was completely filled, as was the wooden gallery before it. Everyone knelt.

Then, amid dead silence, while the wind whispered in the tops of the trees in the glen below, the Father Guardian raised his voice, pronouncing every word distinctly and carefully, as if no syllable should be lost: "*Voce mea ad Dominum clamavi.*"[34] It was the same psalm that Francis recited on his deathbed. The brothers responded, reciting the verses alternately with the Guardian. After the last verse, "*Me expectant justi,*"[35] solemn, impressive silence prevailed again until the voices of all present joined in chanting the beautiful antiphon in honor of St. Francis:

> Hail, holy Father, light of thy country, pattern of the Friars Minor, mirror of virtue, path of justice, rule of life, lead us from the exile of the body unto the kingdom of heaven!

Then the procession filed back to the church, in the tranquil eventide, up the steps, alongside the wall, across the grass-covered ground, the whole scene flooded with the golden radiance of the setting sun. In the twilight of the church where everyone knelt the Litany of the Blessed Virgin was sung, concluding with the hymn of praise that Franciscans often recited centuries ago in honor of the Immaculate Mother of God.

"*Tota pulchra es, Maria,*" chanted the deep voices from one side of the choir.[36]

---

34 "I cried to the Lord." Psalm 142:2 (Ps. 141:2 in Douay-Rheims)
35 "The just wait for me." Psalm 142:8 (Ps. 141:8 in Douay-Rheims)
36 "You are completely beautiful." This is also the title of an antiphon for one of the psalms on the Feast of the Immaculate Conception.

"*Tota pulchra es, Maria*," responded the clear boyish voices on the other side. Thus, they chanted each versicle until the end: "*Intercede pro nobis ad Dominum Jesum Christum.*"[37]

The following morning, which was Sunday, I rose at a very early hour. As I crossed the courtyard of the monastery on my way to the church, the paving stones were still wet with the dew of night. I heard Mass among a crowd of peasants, whose faces were like rough sketches carved in wood of the fathers and novices before the master-hand had begun to finish his work, to idealize and refine the expressions on their faces.

At half-past nine, after standing for a while on the balcony in front of my room, gazing on the lovely view, I left Fonte Colombo. On the grass outside the church and monastery, groups of peasants who had come up for a later Mass were sitting or standing about and chatting. The Father Guardian accompanied me a little way beyond the gate, and then pointed out the distant goals of my next pilgrimages on the other side of the valley—there, the Convent of La Foresta—and beyond it, high up in the mountains, the lonely hermitage of Poggio Bustone.[38]

Then I said farewell, and went on my way down the steep, stony paths into the valley, and up again on the opposite side. All around me the gray mountains rose. In the foreground was the glittering crest of Monte Terminillo, almost the highest in Italy. At a turn in the road, I looked back and took

---

37 "Intercede for us with our Lord Jesus Christ."
38 The location of much of chapter 5 of *Pilgrim Walks*, Poggio Bustone is a *comune*, or municipality, in the Province of Rieti. The word *poggio* means "knoll."

a final glance at Fonte Colombo, with its monastery perched on the highest peak of the thickly wooded mountain. The little bell turret stood out sharply against the sky. In the glen, the river flowed at the foot of the wood which surround the sanctuary: Il Bosco Sacro, "The Holy Wood," the people call it. The atmosphere was warm and soft. I was once more down in the valley, among the habitations of ordinary people.

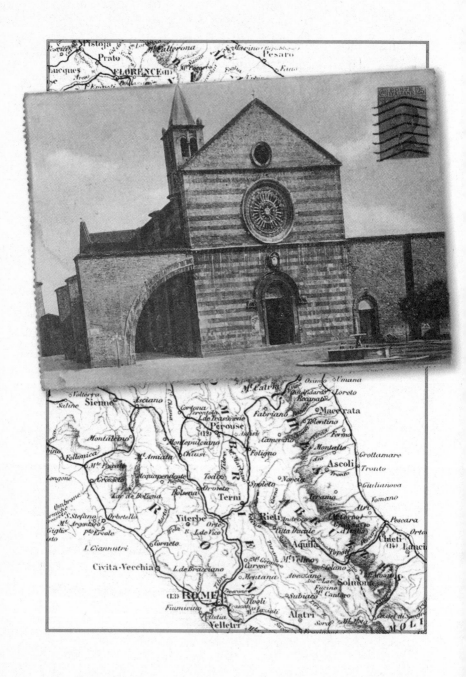

CHAPTER 4

La Foresta

The next goal of my pilgrimage was La Foresta, which is about five miles from Rieti, and is situated in the midst of a beautiful, extensive forest of oaks and chestnuts. This hallowed spot was the scene of the famous miracle of the multiplication of the grapes.[39] It was there I next directed my steps.

It was noon; the sun was scorching; a hot haze rested on the mountains. I left the highroad and took a side-path, following the course of a mountain stream that had hollowed out a bed for itself deep between high earth banks. Then I went through a valley exposed to the full blaze of the noonday sun; in it were leafless oaks and great masses of bluish rock projecting out of the red earth and green grass. The path was a continual ascent.

39 A travel writer in *The New York Times* in 2003 wrote on visiting the four hermitages in the valley of Rieti: "We drove on to La Foresta, a sanctuary eight miles away [from Fonte Colombo] in a sun-drenched valley on the other side of Rieti where the weakening Francis had rested in the summer of 1225 on his way to his eye surgery at Fonte Colombo—and reportedly performed a miracle. So many people crowded around the resident priest's guest house to see Francis that the priest's vineyards were trampled. Francis assured him that he would have a plentiful pressing from the few grapes that were left and according to legend, the priest had his best ever." Linda Bird Francke, "Climbing in St. Francis' Steps," *The New York Times*, Dec. 21, 2003. Available at https://www .nytimes.com/2003/12/21/travel/climbing-in-st-francis-steps.html.

Thinking I must have nearly reached my destination, I inquired of some laborers, and heard that it was still in the distance. The road winds round a mountain, affording extensive views over the plain. At last, I met a kindly peasant who undertook to act as my guide.

The way now led through a forest of oak trees by the side of a sheltered, grass-grown slope. At a turn in the road, my companion pointed out Poggio Bustone, a dark spot among the distant mountains. Then the path grew less steep, and before long we came in sight of a low, much dilapidated wall, behind which was the monastery of La Foresta.

Under the monastery porch, I said goodbye to my guide, and soon the door was opened to me. While the porter took in my letter of introduction, I stood awaiting his return out in the courtyard. It consisted of four covered corridors surrounding a yard flagged with stone, on a somewhat higher level, with a well in the center. Stretching upward above the corridors were four long, high roofs, their red tiles almost bleached by the hot sun, and over them was the deep-blue cloudless vault of heaven.

While I waited there—whether it was due to the fatigue of my long uphill walk or the effect of the burning midday sun, I don't know—a miserable feeling of depression took hold of me. Doubt and despondency filled my mind. All my life, past and present, seemed a hopeless failure—the pursuit of a phantom, an *ignis fatuus*.[40] And yet how great a responsibility rested

40 Literally, "foolish fire," equivalent to "will-o'-the-wisp," meaning: misleading, unreal. An expression referring to light that appears in a swampy place that's not really light, but a natural effect that fools and perhaps frightens us. A frequent expression among early Franciscans, such that it also came to be called "friar's lantern."

on me! Everything grew dark before my eyes and I no longer saw the sunshine that flooded the courtyard of La Foresta. Someone touched me on the shoulder. I startled. An old friar was standing beside me.

Although the silvery hue of his thick hair and full beard indicated old age, his strongly marked, weather-beaten features were lighted up by large, singularly youthful eyes. Those clear brown eyes rested on my face with an expression of truly fatherly kindness, and a pleasant smile played on his lips. He raised his skullcap.

"Father Angelo, at your service," he said.

I grasped the hand he held out to me—a strong, kind, fatherly hand—as a shipwrecked mariner might grasp the hand stretched out to him over the edge of the boat that had come to rescue him.

Father Angelo inspired me at once with the greatest confidence. So, when, a little while later, I was sitting alone with him, I felt no hesitation in pouring out my heart to him, certain that I would find in him a friend, a father who would listen to my troubles and direct me well. I wasn't mistaken. When I had finished my confession and listened to his kindly, wise exhortation, peace, confidence, and courage had returned to my soul. Doubt and difficulty were gone, and when we stepped out again into the courtyard, the sun shone brightly, and above the roofs the sky was blue.

We passed into the garden and stood looking out over the valley. The monastery garden is laid out in terraces on the mountainside—wide, grassy terraces in which red roses and purple rosemary bloom, and where olives, pines, and cypresses raise their crests to the sky. Involuntarily, I lingered in the garden, enjoying the pure air and fresh breeze. But Father Angelo insisted on taking me into the vineyard to show me the old, half-dead vine that is said to date from the time that St. Francis was there. This year it had sent out three small, tender shoots.

From the garden we proceeded to the church, where beneath the altar was the vessel, *la vasca*—the press in which the miraculous grapes were pressed.

"The priest could hardly have made his wine in the church," the old Franciscan said smilingly. "We must suppose that the presbytery stood here originally, and later on it formed part of the church. The legend asserts," he added, "that Pope Gregory IX himself came from Rieti to witness the miracle."

We then went out into the sunshine again. The old friar escorted me through the garden, down one terrace after another. I plucked a few wildflowers that were growing in the grass, and when he saw this, he gathered a bunch of roses and rosemary for me. At the lowest garden gate he wished me farewell, and I went on alone down the stony path. When I had gone a little distance, I turned and looked up. He was standing at the gate, still looking at me. I took off my hat and waved a greeting. Then I saw him returning slowly to the monastery. When he got back up to the door, he turned once more, and I sent him one last salutation, which he returned. Then he went into the house. Goodbye, good Father Angelo, my kind, fatherly friend.

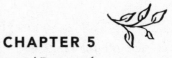

CHAPTER 5

A Sabine Festival

As I pursued my solitary way down the mountain, I soon lost sight of La Foresta and found myself in a wild ravine between massive rocks. A new and curious scene presented itself.

Before me lay a small village in festive garb. I saw a happy crowd and heard the hum of voices. I made my way to the square before the church, where I was surrounded by white headgear, trimmed with lace, and many-colored handkerchiefs and dresses of the peasant women and girls. I had arrived in time for a Sabine popular festival.

I naturally attracted some attention, with my black hat, eyeglasses, and traveling bag. But there was no vulgar, open-mouthed staring. The good people certainly looked at the stranger, exchanged a remark with a neighbor, laughed a little, but then turned their faces again in the direction of the church from which they evidently expected something to come. And, in fact, I soon heard the voice of singing, and out of the semi-darkness of the sacred edifice a banner of Our Lady emerged into the sunlight. It was borne aloft by a stalwart priest and followed by a troop of young girls dressed in white, and then by a crowd of women in the dress of the countryside, looking like a bed of tulips. The men—some tall and slim, others short and thickset—who had been standing somewhat apart, then fell into the ranks, and a procession was formed.

I was just hesitating whether I should join them when the crowd fell back to make way for a sturdy, rosy-faced young man wearing glasses and ordinary clothes. He came up to me and, raising his hat, inquired courteously, with a glance at my bag, if I was wishing to take some photographs. I answered in the negative. "Ah, then," he said, a gleam of intelligence lighting up his features, "you have come for the sake of St. Francis!" I agreed, and we began to talk. He introduced himself to me as the son of the syndic, or mayor, of Poggio Bustone.

"Poggio Bustone is the very place to which I am going!" I exclaimed.

"In that case, I advise you to join the procession here. These people come from Poggio Bustone. They have made a pilgrimage here and are now returning home. Thus, you shall have traveling companions, and will be sure not to lose your way. If you will allow me, I will see that your bag is carried for you."

He took the bag out of my hand and disappeared. In a moment he returned, and then mounted on a magnificent horse, with my bag strapped across his shoulders. The mayor's son was going to take charge of the strange gentleman's property himself! He gave me a kindly nod. Then, with a wave of the hand he made the signal to start, and the procession moved on. It was then past three o'clock.

We proceeded by a narrow, stony path alongside the mountain. I wondered how it was possible to ride on such a road, but the large, well-groomed horse stepped cautiously and surely over the loose stones and masses of rock.

The banner of the Madonna led the way, followed by the girls in white. Then came a crucifix, after which the men walked. Next came a brass band composed of twelve musicians, and finally a long retinue of both sexes. When the music stopped, the girls sang a monotonous, unvarying strain, in which the same refrain came over and over again:

Evivva Maria e chi la creò!
Evivva Maria e chi la creò![41]

All morning, on the way there, they had sung in this fashion, and they continued to do so until we reached Poggio Bustone very late that evening. The distance was thirteen kilometers there, and as many back.

When we had covered a good portion of the way, the mayor's son brought his horse to my side. "Every year," he told me, "when the young girls of the parish make their First Communion, the inhabitants of Poggio Bustone perform this pilgrimage to San Felice. It is not so much a religious festival as a popular festivity, and the municipal authorities provide the music. Consequently, not the clergy but the municipality is represented in it. It is a festival to which the people look forward all year long. Today it has been especially joyous, because it may be that St. Felix has performed a miracle for

41 Lyrics from a popular religious song to the Madonna: "*O Maria quanto sei bella*," "O Mary, how beautiful you are." This repeated line is the most important: "Hurray Mary, and [the One] who created her!"

us."[42] With that, the young man concluded, and he rode ahead to give orders to the musicians.

The rough path led us over hill and valley, between the gnarled stems of silver-gray olives, beneath the oak forest that clothes the slope, across big barren stony fields, then suddenly through fertile valleys where the apple trees were in blossom. As the road sank, the procession displayed itself before me in all its many-colored splendor.

Gradually, I made acquaintance with a few of the pilgrims. Now and then, one came up to me and began to talk, as we walked along the mountainside. Far down at our feet lay the valley of Rieti, half-shrouded in blue haze. Some lakes could be seen glittering in the sunlight through the mist. I was told the names of them, but I have forgotten all except one—the Lake of Piediluco.

Soon we came in sight of a town that was built on successive stages of the mountain. The church steeples rose above the gray roofs of the houses. I asked one of my new friends what was the town's name. He answered, "Cantalice!"

"Not Poggio Bustone, then?"

"It is a long way still to Poggio Bustone," he said with a smile. "You cannot even see it, yet." Then he began to tell me about Cantalice.

"It is a very ancient town, built on the downward slope of the mountain. From one row of houses you can step on to the

---

42 San Felice and St. Felix are one and the same: St. Felix of Cantalice, who lived in the sixteenth century. Born in the Rieti Valley, Felix was a shepherd before joining the Capuchin Franciscans and then became famous for his charity and humility.

roof of another. That old massive tower up high is the fortress in which the inhabitants used to take refuge when an enemy was approaching. Over the gateway is the inscription: *Fides Cantalica me construxit.* 'Cantalice's faithfulness built me.' All the inhabitants joined in the work of building. And the big church on the top of the mountain, with the square in front of it, is San Felice, where St. Felix of Cantalice is buried."

I remembered having seen a picture of that saint—an old man with a white beard carrying a mendicant's bag on his back. On the bag were the words *Deo gratias*, which were frequently on his lips. And now I had come quite unexpectedly to the birthplace of that remarkable man—to Cantalice. We were soon in its streets, and traversing the square, we entered the church where I witnessed a scene that I will never forget.

The mayor's son had hinted, while talking on the way, at a miracle that it was thought San Felice might perform that day. The case was that of a young woman in poor circumstances who had been lame for several years, and whom her father and husband had taken with them on the pilgrimage, in the hope that she might obtain a cure. While on the spot where I first came upon the procession, she imagined that she felt better, and now she was being carried to the saint's burial place, to complete the cure that appeared to have begun.

In a niche behind the altar, over St. Felix's grave, is a gigantic statue of the saint, hung all over with glittering votive hearts. Between the statue and the wall of the choir there is a space about seven feet wide by five feet long. There the sick woman had been brought, and a dense crowd of people had flocked in after her, so that the building was literally packed. Two wax tapers had been lit before the image—of an old, white-bearded man with a kindly smile, tenderly holding in his arms the infant Jesus. Before the statue the invalid was half-sitting, half-kneeling, supported by her gray-haired father and black-haired husband, all three with their eyes fixed entreatingly on the saint. Their prayers were audible and found an echo and response in the multitude.

At first, I did not quite understand it all. I thought that something wonderful had already happened—for just as I came up, I heard the people cry aloud: *Grazie, San Felice!* This expression of thanks was repeated again and again, interrupted by long prayers that the sick woman's old father recited, and which all ended with a fervent, heartfelt: *Grazie, grazie, San Felice!*

After I had been standing there a little while I began to have a clearer notion of what was going on. They were not thanking the saint for what he had already done, but for what they hoped and expected him to do. A moral compulsion, so to speak, was being laid on him, by giving thanks to him beforehand. He could not easily do otherwise than grant their petition.

I pushed my way as far forward as I could—far enough, at any rate, to see the patient. Her eyes had a feverish look. There was a hectic flush on her cheeks. Every now and then, she bent forward and pressed her burning lips to the feet of the saint—the kiss being followed by the supplicating, sorrowful cry: "*O San Felice mio!*" At last, the bystanders began to shake their heads. It was evident that San Felice was not to be persuaded. There was nothing more to be done. He was inexorable. So the vast crowd gradually dispersed; almost all went to join the procession, which was being formed again to proceed on its way.

But the patient, her father, and husband did not give up hope. They left the statue and knelt on the steps of the altar, the old peasant reciting with a trembling voice the Salve Regina—"Hail, holy Queen, Mother of mercy!" After this he said the Litany of Loreto, then a litany to all the saints whose names he knew. And when he had exhausted his repertoire, he wound up with one last bitter cry, in which the flame of hope seemed once more to flare as he called upon San Felice.

When finally we left Cantalice, after having passed through it from top to bottom, it rose above and behind us like a pile of architecture. Just outside town, we halted again. On a bridge over a river, whose bed was at that time dry, refreshment was offered in the shape of cool, rather acid, red wine, served as we sat on the stone balustrade of the bridge.

While the pilgrims were resting, I was introduced to the important leaders of Cantalice. The mayor had driven them out to see the procession. They included the two parish priests of the place, one of whom proved to be well read in Franciscan literature. Later on, I made the acquaintance of the leader of the procession—the stalwart priest whom I saw in

San Felice carrying the banner of the Madonna. He was Don Severino, the archpriest of Poggio Bustone. Finally, up came a broad-shouldered, ruddy-faced countryman, who bowed and introduced himself to me as Nazareno Matteucci. "You must let me put you up for the night," he said, "for I can tell you there is not a single hotel in Poggio Bustone, and the convent is closed. So I always entertain the brothers when they come over to us—from La Foresta, for instance, as well as any strangers who happen to pass this way."

I thanked him for his kind offer but took the occasion to ask the son of the mayor who my new friend was. He gave him an excellent reference. "Nazareno is one of the most prominent peasant proprietors in Poggio Bustone, a respectable and God-fearing man. Two of his sons are Franciscans, and one a Capuchin. A fourth, who is still quite young, is in the seminary. He has two daughters who are Poor Clares, and one other son who is married and lives with his parents."

The road began now to ascend a steep and rugged mountain. Again and again I turned to look back at Cantalice, whose gray houses had assumed a rosy hue in the evening light, while the windows began to glow brightly in the rays of the setting sun. The girls were singing the same strain with renewed energy: "*Evivva Maria e chi la creò!*" Nazareno Matteucci came up to me again and gave me an account of his household, saying that I would feel comfortable, that there was plenty of refinement there. He said he had a brother, Benedetto, who had once studied for the priesthood—"He knows how to talk to a gentleman like you."

The sun had set when we left San Liberato, and in the plain the mist was rising. In the growing darkness we pursued our weary way between stone ramparts, through olive groves, past houses whose inhabitants came out to look at us, and at last, after five hours, the girls in the procession stopped their monotonous song and we came out on a wide road bordered by houses. This was Borgo San Pietro, a suburb of Poggio Bustone.

Before long, we were sitting at supper in Nazareno's house. Beside me sat my host, in his shirt sleeves, with his little granddaughter on his knee. Opposite me was his brother Benedetto, a tall, thin man with a white beard. Last of all, was the married son, a man of about twenty, with small, well-cut features. There were no women at table with us. The woman of the house, Pasqua, waited on us herself. A stout woman, she went back and forth, heavy gold earrings dangling from her ears, her brown wrinkled neck half-hidden by the ample collar of her white bodice.

Pasqua was angry because Nazareno had brought home a guest without letting her know beforehand. He might have sent someone on ahead, riding on a donkey. Now she had nothing to set before the strange gentleman! What would he think of her? Pasqua threw the horn-handled knives down on the tablecloth with such force that they literally danced. Neither of the men, however, seemed to take the least notice of her wrath. Pasqua Matteucci was a good woman, an excellent housewife, a kind mother and grandmother toward her numerous progeny. What did it matter if she blustered a bit? We sat quietly drinking some good wine with our bread.

Benedetto was the main talker. He took hold of me immediately, monopolizing my attention for the whole evening. His nephew wasn't allowed to interpose a word. But suddenly, Benedetto stopped speaking and pointed to his brother. The worthy man, overcome with fatigue, and the unusual amount of wine he had drunk on the way, was fast asleep, his ruddy face bent on his chest. His little granddaughter had slipped off his knee long ago and run to her grandmother in the kitchen.

Benedetto shrugged his shoulders. "That is always the way with Nazareno!" he said. "As soon as one begins to talk about sensible subjects, he drops off to sleep. May blessed Mary—her name be praised forever—protect the man!"

While we talked, we did good justice to the fare Pasqua set before us. Now, I, regardless of the scorn Benedetto expressed for sleepy people, expressed my own wish to go to bed. So I was shown to the guest chamber, which opened out of the room where we had been sitting. It was a spacious apartment with two very high beds, chests of drawers with crocheted covers, a three-legged washstand, a stand with pegs for coats, and scraps of carpet scattered about the stone floor. The windows were fastened inside with a wooden bar, and young Matteucci, who accompanied me carrying a candle, directed my attention to a gun standing by the bedside. "It is loaded," he said, laying an emphasis on the "is."

"Is there any need for that?" I asked.

He smiled, said nothing, but shrugged his shoulders as if to say it was good to be prepared for any emergency.

CHAPTER 6

Poggio Bustone

I AROSE THE NEXT MORNING AT SEVEN. ON ENTERING the dining room, I found Benedetto breakfasting on bread and a glass of wine. Some hot milk was served for me, since coffee is not to be had here among the peasants.

Benedetto and I soon set off on the field path, between green hedges, each carrying a stick. We walked at a good pace, glad to be out in the fresh morning air, under the cloudless sky. "An itinerant life," my companion said, "is the best manner of living. It is the Franciscan life, the apostolic life."

We crossed the dry bed of river, in the midst of which a slender rivulet rippled between big boulders, and soon we reached the archpriest's house on the main street of the Borgo. We found Don Severino somewhat indisposed, due to the long march of the previous day, but he soon got himself ready to come with us. Outside in the street, the mayor's son joined us. He was in everyday clothes, but in every other respect the same as when we saw him last. His blue eyes smiled pleasantly behind gold-rimmed glasses. He, too, was going with us to Poggio Bustone.

It was still a long way to the goal of my journey. The town— of which San Pietro is only a suburb—was five hundred meters above us. Then, one has to cover an equal distance before reaching L'Eremo, St. Francis's hermitage. It is a very long walk, and all the way uphill.

We began to ascend slowly. If one has to climb a mountain, one must not attempt to go quickly. After we'd been walking for a while, we entered one of the first stairway-like streets of Poggio Bustone where children were basking in the warm sunshine. Then we got into a maze of small, steep alleys, all ascending more or less sharply. Everything was stone— houses, steps, streets. Sometimes we walked over huge, rough slabs of stone—that was the rock jutting out into the street. It almost seemed as if the whole town was hewn out of the rock, a mountain peak transformed into human habitations.

We came out onto the market square. There we paused to rest and gaze on the splendid view. Going on, we descended through fresh labyrinths of stone, sunless and chilly. On the steps of the houses, women were sitting at needlework; they looked up and greeted the archpriest as he passed. Then we came to the church—the cathedral of the place. It was being restored. There was nothing of interest about it. While we were inside, the parish priest—a young, good-looking man—came forward with his breviary in hand, wearing a worn-out cassock. We stood talking with him for a while on the steps.

What a strange life it must be for this young priest. Think of living year after year in that poor little place perched on high, intellectually alone with no other society than his breviary, no other solace than the church, no other occupation than baptizing and burying, visiting the sick and hearing confessions, catechizing and preaching. Never so much as a newspaper, and seldom a new book—for his salary is too slender for that. All the long winter—and winter is rigorous in those elevated regions—no other fire than a brazier to warm his numbed fingers before saying Mass. An utter absence of comforts, even less of luxuries, such is life in a presbytery among the Sabine hills.

Today is a gala day for the young priest, since it brings visitors from the lowlands. When we had been standing and talking a while, Don Severino beckoned to one of the boys who stood near and sent him on an errand. The lad soon returned with a bottle of absinthe and some glasses. The liquor was poured, and the little glasses emptied.

Saying farewell to the priest, we resumed our grueling ascent, upward and onward, and soon the town lay far below us. The landscape was spread out at our feet like a map on which blue lakes, green fields, and white roads were plainly marked. All around was silence and absence of life. Now and again we saw a green lizard glide over the sun-warmed rock, and once we stopped to drink from a clear, cool brook flowing past in its stony channel.

We went on climbing higher and higher. The path had turned, and it led over a barren mountain ridge, beneath which the hermitage was built. It was now a perpetual zigzagging of flights of irregular steps. A succession of little chapels stood by the roadside; in one is to be seen a piece of rock bearing the footprint of St. Francis; in another, the impress of his hand; in a third, the depression made by his elbow when he leaned on the rock. Benedetto eagerly pointed out to me these remarkable relics.

"The impression left by his elbow," he explained, "was made when the saint was on his way to Poggio Bustone and rested his head on his hand while looking at the town. He arrived there at three o'clock in the morning. That is why the bells of the town are still rung at that hour on October 4, St. Francis's Day."

At last the path stopped ascending. We went on alongside the great, bluish-gray wall of rock on the summit of the mountain whose highest peak was still many hundred yards above us. Then, at a turn in the path, we came in view of the sanctuary. At the end of the path was a very small chapel—Il Santuario—with a lean-to roof that slopes down from the wall of rock and supports on its extreme edge a modest turret in which a bell is suspended. A few irregular steps—six or seven total—lead up to the door of the chapel.

The chapel is divided into two sections, a lower and an upper. The lower is only a sort of porch from which a staircase ascends, beneath the huge, projecting rock, to the actual grotto, the Hermitage of St. Francis. Over the stairs are the words: *Hic remissa tibi sunt peccata tua sicut postulasti*—"Here your sins [O Francis] were forgiven you as you prayed."[43]

We mounted those narrow stairs, careful to stoop our heads so as not to strike them against the hard rock. A small altar is set up in the grotto; it is a kind of alcove. The altarpiece

---

43 The story of when this happened at Poggio Bustone is told in Part Two of this book.

represents St. Francis in prayer, and Brother Giles asleep. The ground of the chapel is the rock, but the altar is raised on a low wooden platform on which the priest can stand when Mass is said there. We lingered a few moments in devout silence.

Then the mayor's son got up, put his walking stick in a hole in the wall, and rang out a succession of strokes on the bell hanging in the tiny turret. It was exactly noon. He rang the Angelus. The notes sounded far and wide over the valley.

I looked closely at the chapel, the goal of my long journey, before leaving. It consists of only a roof and a wall, in which are three small windows—three little holes—and a cross formed of two round bits of untrimmed branches. Poverty-stricken as the chapel is now, it was even more so when St. Francis knelt there in prayer. Then, the hermitage was nothing but a natural grotto in the mountain, without any roof but the overhanging rock, in the clefts of which a few shrubs grow. In that lonely solitude the saint received the blissful assurance that his sins were forgiven.

It had taken us three hours to come up from Borgo San Pietro. The return journey was accomplished much quicker. It was my intention that afternoon to cross the Rieti Valley to Greccio and go from there by train to Terni.

On reaching Nazareno's house, Benedetto and I dined together. One of the dishes was part of a young lamb, cut up into very small pieces—small mouthfuls—bones, cartilage, meat, all boiled together and served with a piquant sauce. "There is very little nourishment in it. One eats it because it is tasty," said Benedetto with the air of an epicure.

While I was putting my things into my bag, Pasqua came in and looked around. "I am sorry that you are going away so soon, my son," she said. "The socks you took off this morning need mending. I was going to mend them this afternoon." She went with me to the outside flight of stairs; we were talking of the excursion to the chapel that morning. "Yes," she said, "that is a place where the very atmosphere is holy."

I then expressed my thanks for her hospitality and left, asking her to say goodbye for me to Nazareno, who was out on the land. Benedetto accompanied me part of the way, to put me into the right road. After a short distance from the town we said goodbye to each other, but long after his tall form had disappeared behind the acacia hedge of a field path, his hearty, "*Addio, Sor Giovanni mio!*" rang in my ears.

The road quickly took me down into the low-lying land. The apple trees were in full bloom. The birds were singing. Children were playing in front of the houses. The bean fields were in flower and the air was full of their fragrance. Again and again I turned and looked back. I could not discern Nazareno Matteucci's house among the many other farmhouses at the foot of the olive-grown hill. The old gray town stood out prominently. However, on the height above rose the bare, uncultivated mountain with patches of purple forest, covered by paths of a reddish hue. The hermitage was not to be seen from where I stood. It lay in a recess of the mountain. Only a corner of the wood above it was visible.

I walked on and on, farther and farther out into the wide-open country. Before me the town of Greccio was in full view. In fact, for some time the road led directly toward it. But then it turned in the direction of Rieti. I had to ask my way.

In the company of three or four workmen, I took a shortcut along a narrow path leading to a river, over which we were ferried by a sturdy young woman. One of the men helped her to manage the sail, and when we reached the other side, paid her for his passage with a kiss. My companions and I went to a tavern, near the station at Greccio, for a drink. It happened to be just after the time of leaving work. The tavern was full of workmen and other nondescript individuals. All were, however, well-behaved and even polite. When I had paid for one bottle of red wine, my companions insisted on providing a second, but they would not accept my offer of a third. Then we parted company. I returned to the station, and paced up and down on the platform, looking up to the dark mountains where a few lights were visible and where I knew my friends in the monastery were assembled for night prayers. Suddenly the curfew bell rang from the heights. I felt almost as if my home were there.

It was midnight when I reached Foligno. I got someone to show me the way to my hotel; it was only a few steps through a wide avenue lighted with electric light. Before long, I was in a comfortable bed, and had forgotten all my weariness in a sound slumber.

CHAPTER 7
Assisi

The next morning, I visited the tomb of Blessed Angela of Foligno in the Franciscan church of that town. Her remains are enclosed in a magnificent sarcophagus, the sides of which are plated with gold. Afterwards, I took myself to the residence of the cathedral canons and made acquaintance with Monsignor Faloci, of literary renown—a small, slim priest whose smooth face and regular features are the essence of Italian.[44] I presented him with a copy of my Danish translation of the *Fioretti*, and he in return gave me his Life of St. Clare of Montefalco, the best biography of her yet published.

In the afternoon, I resumed my pilgrimage.

By the time the train reached Spello, where it stopped a while, the sky had become overcast and the mountains were shrouded in mist. Before long, I caught sight of an outline in the distance, strongly marked against the gray sky: the familiar outline of the mountain above Assisi, on the summit of which stands St. Clare's castle. In another minute the whole town came into view, a clearly defined line of buildings at the foot of Mount Subasio.

44 Monsignor Michele Faloci Pulignani was a popular priest and author in Foligno. In addition to his book mentioned on St. Clare, Msgr. Faloci edited an important edition of the *Legend of the Three Companions* (1898), and he sought to revive devotion to the fourteenth-century Blessed Tomasuccio of Foligno.

As we proceeded, I saw the fissure at Carceri, and in the midst of the green vineyards the pointed gable and spire of the little church of Rivo Torto. Then, way in the background, I saw the church in which St. Francis is interred, and the big monastery beside it.[45] I recognized the towers of Assisi one after another: the tower and dome of the cathedral up above; the tower on the piazza lower down, with the spires and towers of Santa Maria del Vescovado; the Chiesa Nuova; and others.

Leaving the train station, I set off immediately toward the ivory-like buildings of the Franciscan monastery that gleamed in the evening light. A strong, sweet smell was wafting to me from the flowery meadows as I passed by. In the distance were the mountains of Perugia. I remembered it all so well from a previous visit some ten years earlier.

On I went, past Casa Gualdi, the place where St. Francis, when dying, gave his last blessing to Assisi; past the little Gothic chapel to the right of the road, where a lamp burns before an image of the Madonna; up the small steep flight of steps leading to the city gate, where, leaning on the parapet, I gazed out over the landscape, the vast plain shut in by violet-hued mountains bathed in the golden radiance of the setting sun. Passing on, I soon found myself before the church and monastery of San Francesco.

When I entered the church, it was almost dark within the broad, low nave. The windows, with their saints in bright and

---

45 Subasio, Rivo Torto, Carceri, these are all essential places from the biography of St. Francis. See *The Road to Assisi: The Essential Biography of St. Francis*, and others.

varied colors, looked as if set with jewels. I went up to and past the high altar where some lay brothers were cleaning and arranging the furniture, and I turned into the south transept to look again at the familiar frescoes. Then I peeped into the sacristy and saw the dark carved oak chests and presses, all exactly the same as I saw them ten years before. I felt as if I were in a dream—a delightful dream from which I didn't want to awake.

Before leaving the church, I went down into the crypt, feeling my way in the darkness with hand and foot, until I stood before the railing that surrounds the tomb of the saint, where flickered a number of little lamps. In the profound tranquility of that hallowed spot I realized that I was really again in Assisi, with which I associated so many happy memories and holy aspirations.

Passing later by St. Clare's Church, built of red and white stone, I went down the road bordered by olive trees to San Damiano. The church was quite dark, because it was now eventide; yet there was light enough for one to see Tiberio of Assisi's fresco in the little chapel in the courtyard—a charming harmony of pale, subdued tints. I sat down to rest for a few minutes on the bench outside the convent gate. The sunset sky showed golden between the delicate gray leaves of the olive trees. Two aged friars came slowly down the road. They knocked at the gate and were admitted.

I wandered about the town for some time longer, sauntering through the long, lonely avenues, where only here and there a solitary lamp shed a feeble light, and climbing the narrow, steep streets before taking myself back to my night quarters. The streets were quiet and almost deserted. Everything seemed unchanged.

Early the next morning, I was awakened by the sound of bells ringing in the cool morning air. Looking from my window, I saw below the moss-covered roofs of the town, still wet with dew, and the church of San Pietro. Somewhat later, I took the same way that I had followed on the day before—the road leading to San Damiano.

There was something exhilarating about the early hours of that sunny May morning. Between the olive trees the corn stood already half high, a bright, rich green, and the olive leaves were of a fresher color than in summer. Everything looked so fresh, so full of life, in the bright scene before me, so that, on arriving at San Damiano I couldn't resolve to go into the church at once to look at antiquities and relics. I thought I would walk along the field paths for a little while, under the trees on the hillside.

As I went, I met an old Franciscan pacing up and down in the sunshine, his breviary in his hand, keeping the place with his thumb while his admiring gaze was fixed on the clear blue heavens. Our eyes met and the old father smiled in his long, gray beard, a smile that beamed with good nature, and without preamble he exclaimed, *"Che bello cielo!"* ("What a lovely sky!")

I stopped, and we talked. With the garrulity of old age, he talked at length about the beauty of nature, declaring it to be the best of temples in which to worship, praise, and magnify the God of creation. Then he wished me a courteous farewell and passed on his way, while I entered the cool, shady little church, resolved to see everything there that remembers St. Francis and St. Clare, those two who were one in spirit and whose lives were ones of prayer, poverty, and praise.

The Sisters of St. Clare no longer dwell in the poor convent at San Damiano. (It is now inhabited by brothers.) But higher up, close to the Porta Nuova, is the large church erected by Philip da Spoleto in the middle of the thirteenth century not long after the basilica over the grave of St. Francis was completed. It was there, accordingly, that I sought for further memorials of San Damiano. I saw the Byzantine crucifix whose mute eloquence appealed so forcibly to Francis's youthful heart, and was so decisive for his whole life, that from that time forward it was said of him that he bore the wounds of the Lord Jesus in his heart.

I also saw a notable relic and precious heirloom of St. Francis—the breviary that Brother Leo wrote for him, and as an inscription in the book informs you, out of which "as long as his health permitted, he used to recite the Office in accordance with the regulations of the Rule; and when he was no longer well enough to recite it himself, he desired to have it read in his presence, and this was done as long as he lived. After that, Brother Angelo and Brother Leo earnestly begged the Lady Benedicta, abbess of this convent of St. Clare, and all who would succeed her, to keep and preserve forever with the utmost care this book that our Father so often made use of, in pious remembrance of him." This request has been fulfilled. The breviary, created on beautiful parchment in Brother Leo's elegant penmanship, is preserved to this day under lock and key in a doubly secure reliquary.

From St. Clare's church I went down below into the crypt, a place that, like San Francesco, is a scene of interment. Ever since 1850, when the spot where she was buried was discovered and the crypt was built, the body of St. Clare, undecomposed by the lapse of centuries, has been able to be seen by every visitor. A curtain is drawn aside, a wax taper is held by a sister, and behind an iron railing, fronting a large square of glass is seen the form of the saint, beautiful in her last long sleep.[46] "*Clara nomine, vita clarior, clarissima moribus,*" says Thomas of Celano. "Bright in name, more brilliant in life and character."

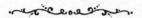

There was still much to be seen in and around Assisi.

I spent one afternoon taking a long walk over Mount Subasio to Carceri, the secluded monastery situated in a laurel-filled cleft in the mountains where Brother Rufino was seriously tempted by the devil in the form of the Crucified. The following morning, I visited Rivo Torto, down below on the plain, and Portiuncula, which lies close to the train station.

---

46 As always, remember that he is describing each scene as it was in the early twentieth century.

Rivo Torto is the place where Francis dwelt with his earliest disciples after his return from Rome when Innocent III had given his sanction to their manner of life. Their habitation was a mere shed; there was so little space in it that there was hardly room for everyone to sit down. To prevent confusion, and so that each person might know his place, Francis wrote the names of the brothers in chalk on the boards. They had neither church nor chapel; the brothers erected a large wooden cross before the shed and around it they used to kneel in prayer. It is probably in remembrance of this that a large cross always stands before Franciscan houses.

They had no means of subsistence unless they could obtain employment by helping the peasants in field work. Provisions would be given them in payment for their labor. Often, these penitents of Assisi, as they styled themselves, returned empty-handed from their begging expeditions, and then they had to be satisfied with turnips instead of bread, water instead of wine. To us it seems a hazardous undertaking on Francis's part to embrace such rigorous poverty, and one often wonders how ten or twelve men could live this way, without bread to eat, a fire to warm themselves, or books to read. Yet the annals of the Order record only one desertion among the first disciples: Brother John of the Hat, so-called because he objected to wearing the cowl that forms part of the habit of the Order.

Leaving Rivo Torto, I took the straight road to Portiuncula— or, as the place is now called, Santa Maria degli Angeli. There in the large, light church, and in the monastery adjoining it, are all the well-known relics and hallowed spots: the original chapel of the Portiuncula, which Francis built with his own hands; the cell in which he died, and where over the altar is now Luca della Robbia's statue of the saint; and near the entrance, Pisano's painting on the lid of the saint's coffin. Then there is the rose garden where the bushes are strangely flecked as if with spots of blood; and the chapel erected over St. Francis's cell, decorated with frescoes from the brush of Lo Spagna and Tiberio d'Assisi.[47]

In the sacristy the usual souvenirs of the place were offered to me for purchase, and while I was there I met the young Padre Alberto, Nazareno Matteucci's son from Poggio Bustone, to whom I had sent word that I was there. He came up to meet me with a look of inquiry in his large brown eyes—a slight, strikingly handsome young man. I grasped his hand and said I was the bearer of many kind greetings from his home—from Nazareno, Pasqua, Uncle Benedetto, Don Severino, and the mayor's son, Signor Provaroni. At each name I mentioned he opened his eyes wider. At last he burst out, saying, "But who are you, then?" and his eyes were filled with tears. All of Poggio Bustone, his home, was suddenly brought before him.

Still, it is perhaps unbecoming of a Franciscan friar to stand in public crying like a child. So, pulling himself together, Padre Alberto took hold of my sleeve and drew me into the refectory. "Come!" he said, "Have you dined? Ah, that is a pity. But a glass of wine?" And he hurried to his place at the table and took some of the wine that had been put there for him to drink at supper. His hand shook as he poured out

---

47 Giunta Pisano (ca. 1200–1260); Giovanni di Pietro, aka Lo Spagna "the Spaniard" (1450–1528); Tiberio d'Assisi (ca. 1470–1524).

a glass for me, and tears were still falling from his long dark eyelashes. All of Poggio Bustone was so far away from him, and yet so near to his heart. And here was a stranger who had seen everyone there just a few days ago, and who seemed to bring with him the very atmosphere of home. What a strange thing life is, and how easily the heart is touched.

Before long, I left the monastery and the church and was seated outside one of the little inns opposite the large basilica, which is of the Renaissance period, that St. Pius V caused to be built over Brother Francis's simple little chapel. And while the day drew to a close and the sun shed its golden radiance over the scene, with a big fountain alongside the wall of the church splashing down, I sat and pondered.

At half-past three the next morning I went with my worthy host from the hotel the short distance to the station. It was a dark, warm morning. My host carried a lighted candle in his hand. There was not even a breath of wind to make it flicker. We reached the station and the train arrived almost immediately. I got into a coach crowded with night travelers—a mixed company of not altogether desirable companions. As I sat by the window, I watched Assisi disappear from sight, a dark silhouette with three solitary lights.

I hadn't slept much that night. In the evening, not long after the Angelus rang, just as I had been thinking I should go to rest early, the bells of Assisi had struck, calling me in their festive notes, jubilant yet solemn. San Francesco's bells went on ringing and ringing. Up there on the hill stood San Francesco's convent with all its windows lit up, and almost before I knew what I was doing I was on my way there. I felt I must go up once more to Assisi. I must once more experience the singular, intoxicating charm of those streets, those steep alleys, those unpaved ways and open squares.

So on and on I went until I got up there and could wander about everywhere unnoticed and unknown, visiting all the spots that were so dear to me: the square in front of Santa Chiara; the road with the wide vista of the open country beyond the Porta Nuova; the steep and narrow alley leading up to Sant'Andrea; all the localities rich in memories and associations, all of which I was to leave behind me the following morning, and which I would perhaps never revisit.

Once more I passed by the green gate of St. Philomena's little convent, and lingered before the grating, thinking of the brothers who were calmly reciting their Latin night prayers within, as they would do the next day when I would no longer be there, and as they would do should I return there sometime or other many years later.

After a while, I tore myself away. At the corner where the high road to Assisi turns off to the church and monastery, I sent back a last lingering look. High up above I saw under an arch in the wall the swinging lantern whose light had often shone on me when I sat at my window listening to the conflicting voices within me. Only one woman, dressed in black, came noiselessly down the narrow, deserted street, and I heard the purling of the brook. Farewell, Assisi—*Assisi mio*, farewell!

In a state of exaltation, I walked the long way from Assisi back to Portiuncula. The night air was scented with flowers. The sky was spangled with innumerable stars. The bells of Assisi were silent, but the light in the windows was still visible behind me. Again and again I could not stop looking back. Again and again I felt I must repeat my goodbyes. Even when I had returned to my room at the hotel, I looked out for one last sight of the tremulous lights of Assisi. Farewell, city of a thousand memories.

And now here I am seated in the train speeding northward toward Terontola.[48] We reached Perugia just at daybreak. Four working men with big bundles got in; they seemed very jolly and merry. They talked and shouted noisily, threw their packages down, lighted cigars. *"Addio, Perugia!"* the oldest and most jovial of them called out when the train began to move out of the station. The words had hardly escaped his lips when he burst into tears, sobbing with his head against the window frame. The others tried to comfort him. "He is going away from his children," his friends said to us. They were immigrants going to Nice.

I got off at Cortona. I wanted to visit the town which St. Margaret[49] made famous. I also wished to see the Franciscan monastery of Celle nearby.

---

48 On the shores of Lake Trasimeno, just after Umbria has turned into Tuscany.

49 An Italian penitent of the Third Order who lived from 1247–1297. She pursued a life of penance and prayer in Cortona and opened a hospital there for the ill and the homeless, establishing a congregation of tertiary sisters who vowed to care for those who came there. She recounted hearing the voice of Jesus in prayer, and she was known to criticize the bishop of Arezzo, which contained Cortona, for his worldly ways. See chapter 8, below.

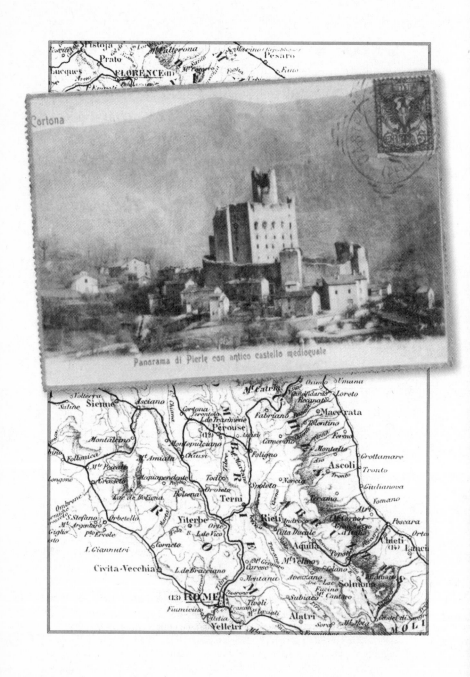

Panorama di Pierle con antico castello medioevale

CHAPTER 8
Cortona,
on the Way to La Verna

From below, Cortona looks very pleasing, with St. Margaret's Church standing out conspicuously on the highest point. It is a modern structure but built in an old architectural style of black and white marble. The town is, however, unclean and full of beggars and idlers.

Soon after midday I set out for Celle.[50] It is one of the very oldest settlements of the Franciscan Order. The day was warm. A hot haze brooded over the wide valley of Chiesa, marked out as it was into vineyards, dotted with cypresses, intersected by white roads. Blue mountains rose in the distance. I heard the cuckoo's cry, and happy butterflies flitted past me.

Now the monastery of Celle (the Cells) is inhabited today by Capuchin friars, and popular parlance has given their name to the place. One must not ask in Cortona the way to Celle: one must ask the way to *I Cappuccini*. It struck me as one of the most peculiar, fantastic spots I had ever visited.

At the bottom of a deep fissure in Monte Sant'Egidio rushes a turbulent river, spanned in several places by stone bridges with bold arches. The old convent, situated on both

---

50 The Convent of Le Celle ("the cells") or *Convento delle Celle*, where St. Francis probably resided briefly, perhaps as early as 1211. The infamous Brother Elias also spent time there, mostly after he was deposed as minister-general of the Order. He is thus known as Brother Elias of Cortona.

sides of the chasm, consists of a small number of scattered houses rising one above another on different shelves of rock, with gardens in which the friars may be seen walking about or working busily. Everywhere are steps, balustrades, terraces, gable-ends, bell-turrets, and trees. And on the eminence above rises a forest of ilexes and dark, pointed cypresses.

A zigzagged path, roughly paved with large, uneven slabs of stone, leads down to the bottom of the chasm where you cross one of the bridges. Greenish waters of a rapid river rush by noisily. Then you ascend again on the opposite side, until at last you come to an open green—the space before the monastery—where a traditional cross stands. The entrance to the church and to the house are under a projecting roof of a rather low lean-to, in one corner of which is a stone table surrounded by stone benches. I am told these are for the accommodation of the inhabitants of Cortona who make excursions there on Sundays, outfitted with luncheon baskets.

The most noteworthy thing about Celle is its peculiar situation, for there are not many memories of St. Francis there. A black-bearded Capuchin wearing glasses, with particularly regular white teeth, showed me the little that there was to be seen: the cell where St. Francis used to pray. It was a cold, damp, dismal room with one loophole of a window looking out over the brawling river and the naked rock. One of the walls was decorated with a painting of the Madonna in Byzantine style.

Then I left Celle. It had begun to rain. A mechanic, with whom I entered into conversation along the way, took me by a shortcut across the mountain to St. Margaret's Church. We were wet all through by the time we got there. It was already almost dark in the church. The kindly, brown-habited Franciscans were most cordial in their reception. They did what they could for us, and showed us everything: here was the cell of St. Margaret, which in her day stood on the bare rocky hill above the town; there hung the crucifix that spoke to her; and there, on the back of her sarcophagus over the high altar was her portrait painted by Pietro da Cortona—a faithful representation of her body after death, exactly as it still remains uncorrupt down to this day.

Could we see her remains? No, no one is allowed to do that. The municipal authorities of Cortona have had a lock put on the shrine and will not give up the key. Quite recently a visitor came with a letter of recommendation from Cardinal Ferrari, but it got him nowhere: he had to go back where he came from. It is of course nothing but officious meddling—the mayor is a liberal and doesn't care a bit about St. Margaret— but likes to annoy us by keeping her under lock and key. So said my guide.[51]

From the church the cheerful young father—his name was Cherubino; he teaches philosophy to the young Franciscans pursuing their studies there—took us into the refectory where

51 At about the same time this was written, Br. Louis Baldwin, OFM, provincial of the Irish Friars Minor, wrote: "The City of Cortona, the Cortona of to-day, is to the memory of our great Franciscan Magdalen, in some degree, what Assisi is to the memory of St. Francis: Cortona is, indeed, the City of Margaret." Letter of commendation, frontmatter, *St. Margaret of Cortona: The Magdalen of the Seraphic Order*, Rev. Leopold de Cherance, OSFC, trans. R. F. O'Connor (New York: Benziger Brothers, 1903), vi.

a large crowd of fathers and brothers gathered around us. We chatted about all manner of things with them while taking some refreshment.

When we emerged on to the windswept green grass in front of the church, the rain had stopped. The air was cold and wonderfully pure and invigorating. Darkness had closed in. The lamps were lighted in the town below. Father Cherubino kindly accompanied us a short distance, but the way down was not difficult to find. Soon we reached Cortona itself. Through steep, rain-washed streets we got into the center of the town.

At the marketplace I took leave of my companion.

"Goodbye, sir," he said, adding, *"Ci vedremo in cielo!"* ("We'll see each other in heaven!")

The next morning, I was up by five o'clock, and on my way to Mount La Verna, in the Casentino Valley, somewhat south of Florence.

CHAPTER 9
The Holy Mountain

The Franciscan monastery on Mount La Verna[52] is an extensive complex, comprising several different structures erected over the course of seven centuries. A stranger soon learns to distinguish the principal parts. First there is La Chiesina, a church dating from the latter half of the thirteenth century, corresponding to the chapel constructed by Count Orlando's orders, under the title of Santa Maria degli Angeli, for St. Francis and his brothers. Then there is Chiesa Maggiore, the principal church, in the form of a cross, in the simple and noble style of the fourteenth century, enriched with as many as six of Della Robbia's best paintings. Then a monastery, in front of which is a small space flagged with stone, from which one has a far-reaching view of the majestic mountain scenery. And finally, there is the Chapel of the Stigmata, erected in 1263 on the spot where St. Francis received the marks of Christ's sacred wounds on September 14, 1224. This chapel is situated a considerable distance from the monastery and other buildings, but still connected to it in a covered way.

---

52 Mount Penna is the actual topographical name for the mountain upon which sits the Franciscan basilica and sanctuary, La Verna. But "Mount La Verna" is not uncommon.

Twice every twenty-four hours—in the afternoon after Vespers, and in the night after Matins—the friars wind their way to the Chapel of the Stigmata to commemorate the wondrous miracle. They do not keep silence as they go. The walls re-echo the voice of prayer and praise, and when they reach the chapel they kneel down and recite this antiphon in honor of St. Francis:

Signasti hic, Domine, servum tuum Franciscum signis redemptionis nostrae.

O Lord, here you marked Francis your servant with the signs of our redemption.

While singing, two of the friars point to the stone in front of the high altar, which marks the exact spot where St. Francis knelt where he received the sacred stigmata.

On that rainy day in May when I arrived at La Verna, the afternoon procession was long over, so I begged the guest-master to find me before Matins the next morning. I wanted this particularly because I was not sure whether I could spend another night on the mountain.

While we were talking about it, two other friars came into the guest room. One of them introduced himself to me as the Father Guardian, Father Saturnino da Caprese. The other was one of the Franciscans recently expelled from France,[53]

53 The French Third Republic, which began in 1870, was hostile to the Catholic Church, particularly its religious orders and priests. There were various smaller persecutions and then, in 1907, a decree dispossessed the Franciscans of their monastery in Cimiez, Nice, expelling them from the country. Also, interestingly: Fr. Saturnino da Caprese was the author in 1902 of an Italian guidebook to La Verna, *Guida illustrata della Verna.* There's a copy at the Library of Congress.

named Father Samuel—or, as the Italians, with their fondness for doubling the final consonant, called him, *Samuelle*. The Father Guardian left almost immediately, but when Fr. Samuel discovered that I could speak French he was delighted and sat with me talking for quite some time. Finally, he promised to call me at night in time for the procession.

The fear of being late, however, made me so uneasy that I began to wake up long before the time. At one o'clock in the morning I started up, and in the pitch-darkness groped around for the lucifer matches on the table by my bedside. I struck one: it spluttered, smoked, threw off sparks, and burned with a blue flame. Then I was able to light a candle with it.

I didn't dare go to sleep again. I left the candle burning; its faint light only made more perceptible the darkness of the large, deathly cold room. And while I lay there in the intense loneliness and silence, not hearing even the patter of rain outside, an appalling dread took over—a dread worse than that of death—the most awful fear that can weigh an unhappy mortal to the ground: the fear that he might, after all, not be the friend of God.

Why, I asked myself, should this fear fall on me here of all places—at La Verna, where I had so often longed to direct my pilgrim steps! Then a voice answered—a harsh, hard, ugly voice, which I had heard before, and in which there was not the least accent of sympathy: "Don't you know that there are some to whom God gives all in this world because he can give them nothing in the next? That he lets them have their will here because there is no joy for them hereafter? And if one finds pleasure in pilgrimages and religious feelings, in pious thoughts and the relics of saints, God grants his desires and allows him to enjoy the sweets of piety as others enjoy art, honors, or dissipation. Such a one is not really nearer to God than those others, nor does he have a better chance for heaven."

The loud, sharp notes of a bell interrupted my dreadful musing. I got up, dressed quickly, and went into the corridor outside my room. A little farther on I came to a flight of stairs that took me down into a yard. There I struck another match, and by its feeble, uncertain light, I thought I saw, a few steps off, a huge creature—a gigantic bulldog or mastiff standing motionless, ready to pounce on me.

Without uttering a sound, I quickly retreated, with the same hateful voice in my ear: "That is the Evil One waiting for you."

But this time I heeded the voice. I found my cell and quietly fetched my candle. I went up the stairs: was there a way out up above? But I only got into an attic full of all sorts of rubbish. Then I began to explore the corridor slowly and systematically. First, I put a chair to the door to keep it open, for there was no latch outside, only a keyhole without a key. I knocked at all the doors in the corridor but got no answer. On the opposite side there was nothing but windows opening on to the courtyard. At last, at the far end of the corridor I found a little door which was evidently the way out. It too was locked! I shook it in vain. I was locked in, a helpless prisoner.

Then the bells rang for the second time—a prolonged, joyous peal. I thought despairingly, *Now the procession will start and I will not be there to see it. They have forgotten me. Or, perhaps, in mistaken kindness, they've left me to sleep, thinking I can go with them tomorrow night.* Despair gave me strength.

I rattled the door furiously and knocked until I woke the echoes. The friars were surely in the church and couldn't hear me. Then came the bells ringing again, for the third time. How musical, how happy they sounded!

I leaned against the window, staring out into the dark night, where not the faintest streak of dawn was visible.

All at once I saw a light in the windows of the opposite building. The light moved. There was someone over there carrying a candle, coming nearer. One window after another was lighting up in my direction. Soon I saw a figure walking along the corridor which must lead to the locked door behind which I was standing. My heart leaped with joy. They had not forgotten me.

A key rattled from the other side of the door, a bolt was drawn back, and there stood Father Samuel smiling and kind, his glasses glittering in the candlelight.

"I am not too late?" I asked anxiously.

The good father seemed somewhat surprised to find me in such a hurry. "By no means," he answered. "There is plenty of time. We have only just finished Matins, then come Lauds, and the procession is not until they are ended."

What a relief! I followed him in silence through the long, dark passages. When we got to a high door with iron clamps, he blew out the candle and we entered the church. It was so cold, I shivered.

The lofty, vaulted roof was lost in shadow. Behind the high altar the apse was brilliantly lighted. The friars were reciting the Office in the usual manner, on one note, in measured time. I listened a while and caught the words of the *Benedicite*. My agitation began to subside, my fears calmed as the praises of the Almighty God fell on my ears. Other equally beautiful psalms of praise followed; then came the *Benedictus*, at the close of which a lay brother came out of the choir down into the church with a lantern. He threw the doors wide open, and from behind the altar the procession slowly proceeded. First, two lanterns were carried, swinging from high poles. Then followed in long succession the friars in their brown habits, walking two by two. I counted them: there were thirty-seven in all.

I joined the procession. Someone in front began to recite Psalm 51: "*Miserere mei Deus.*" ("Have mercy on me, O God.") The voices of the others arose in response: "*Et secundum multitudinem miserationum tuarum, dele iniquitatem meam.*" ("According to the multitude of Thy mercies, do away mine offences.")—words which found an echo in my heart.

By this time, we had reached the church door. The boundless night outside—the gray, foggy night—lay like a shroud on the broad, bleak, lonely landscape. The wind blew on us icily cold. The fog rolled like waves of vapor in the light of the lanterns. But we soon turned away from the dark night and entered the covered way on the right. The long line of friars walked on quickly before me, their shadows flitting over the dark, cold walls.

When the *Miserere* ended, the *De Profundis* was recited. Meanwhile, we had arrived at a trellised door in the right wall of the passage, and after going down a few steps we came into the antechamber of the Chapel of the Stigmata. A kneeling chair was placed for me exactly before the entrance to the chapel, within which the brothers had already taken their places, filling the choir stalls with some kneeling on the steps of the altar. Above them was an altarpiece in blue and white, a copy of a crucifixion by Della Robbia.

The service in the chapel was quite short. The antiphon, as I expected, was chanted; then followed a few minutes of silent prayer. After this one of the friars began to intone a litany, and each and all prostrated full length before the altar and kissed the ground. Then we returned to the church, the litany being recited along the way.

When it was ended, Father Samuel came and conducted me out. As the door closed behind me I heard a noise in the church: the brothers were beginning to scourge themselves. The good French father left me at the door of my room, after wishing me a courteous *"Bonne nuit!"* ("Good night!") It was nearly two o'clock. I went to bed again and slept soundly until eight.

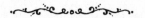

While I was asleep, a beautiful, bright spring morning had dawned, flooding Mount La Verna with golden light. From the little terrace in front of the church and convent I could see a wide panorama of wild, picturesque scenery. Leaning over the edge of the parapet, I could look down into an abyss of wet rocks; and far, far below them lay the verdant fields, with huge boulders here and there. Those were the open fields I had crossed on the previous evening, in the pelting rain, on my way to the mountain. I could trace the road by which I had come.

Then, up came Father Samuel, fresh and bright as the morning. Together, then, we visited every spot hallowed by association with St. Francis: the cave where he prayed, the other cave where he slept, and, high up on the mountain, the grotto in which Brother Leo was accustomed to say Mass for his master and spiritual father.

After we made a long and difficult descent, we stood for a while in silence at the bottom of the dark, damp ravine between gigantic walls of rock where St. Francis lived. I could not refrain from saying that I could not imagine anyone living in such a spot, so often exposed to the weather like we had yesterday.

"True," Father Samuel answered, "the climate of La Verna is very inclement for the greater part of the year. We have three, or at most, four months of summer. The rest of the year we have snow, rain, fog, and storms. I have heard visitors who came from Assisi say that what they had seen there is not to be compared with what we have here. Assisi is lovely, pleasing, delightful; there our Institute is seen in its fairest growth. But here one sees where its roots are struck, the depths out of which it cries to God. Here its aspect is indeed appalling. Nothing else can be said of it."

Ascending by a narrow flight of steps between colossal masses of rock, we reached Brother Leo's cell, which is light and airy. At the farthest end is a small altar, before which there is room for only the officiating priest to stand.

"I said Mass up here once," observed Father Samuel, as if answering my yet unspoken question. "It was on a summer morning, exactly at the hour of sunrise. Just as I made the sign of the cross before beginning, the crimson beams of the sun shone out over that distant mountain, Monte Casella. And when I turned to say the *Dominus vobiscum*, what a glorious sight the side landscape presented! The sun's rays were darting out to dispel the morning mist! I was so overcome by the thought of God's greatness that I scarcely dared to take his name upon my lips, and every time that I came to the word *Dominus* or *Deus* in the Mass I hesitated and trembled, like the children of Israel at the foot of Sinai. And I banished every thought of earth out of my mind, as Moses removed his shoes from his feet in the presence of the burning bush. Truly, this the place to say, *Sursum corda!*—'Lift up your hearts!'"

As we descended the slope he continued: "Yes, La Verna is called the Franciscan Calvary, and rightly so, because the Crucifixion was renewed, repeated in a marvelous way, on Francis's body. It might also be called our Tabor, the Mount of Transfiguration, because Francis was never so near heaven as during those lonely hours on Mount La Verna. It is easier for us weak ones to follow him to Tabor than to Calvary.

"St. Francis loved this mountain more than any other. He was one who attached himself to places, and in no place did he experience such emotion as when he was leaving La Verna for the last time. Have you seen his touching words of farewell? I will read them to you this afternoon. They are very beautiful. We read them in the refectory every year on September thirtieth, the anniversary of Francis's departure from here."[54]

The morning hours sped by quickly. The time for the High Mass drew near. We turned our steps toward the church. After the Mass I dined with a bright-eyed young peasant, little more than a boy, who had come to La Verna *per farsi frate*—"to become a friar." He was about to exchange his secular clothes for the brown habit and cowl.

After dinner I climbed the mountain above the monastery. The summit reaches the same height as Vesuvius. There the mountain is thickly wooded. On the extreme edge are some majestic beeches, and below them is gray rock carpeted with blue anemones, yellow cowslips, and small purple hyacinths. In the interior of the wood the ravines are shaded by a thick growth of Scotch firs. The clouds, which had looked threatening, began to roll away over the majestic mountains, and the sun shone with such heat—almost summer heat— that the ground was dry enough for me to sit down upon a rock. There I stayed until the bells rang for Vespers.

54 September 30, 1224, two years and a few days before Francis died.

After Vespers the second procession of the day wended its way to the Chapel of the Stigmata, with a longer following, but without the impressive solemnity of the nocturnal one.

Toward evening I went in search of Father Samuel to remind him of his promise to read me St. Francis's farewell. It was a transcript of the original document, which is written on parchment, penned by Brother Masseo, and preserved in the reliquary of the monastery. After reading it the good father talked to me for a long time—or, rather, delivered a discourse on the intense love of the saint for God—a love which, for God's sake, he extended to all his creatures. At last he stopped and said:

"But, my dear sir, here I sit and let my tongue run on, forgetting how tired you must be. Please pardon me. I so seldom have an opportunity to speak my own language, it makes me almost feel as if you were a fellow countryman. What time do you start tomorrow morning? At five o'clock? Very well. At four-thirty I will be in the church to say my Mass, and you must not leave without that blessing."

He then wished me a hearty good night. Soon I was alone in my cell. I went to the window. The sky was overcast, the beeches and firs of La Verna silhouetted black against gray heavens. I stood for a long time looking out. This was the end of my pilgrimage. Starting from Rome, passing through the Rieti Valley, through Assisi and Cortona, I had reached La Verna. The crib of Greccio had led me to the mystical crucifixion on La Verna.

PART
TWO

Francis of Assisi *From*

When Francis hears "Your sins are forgiven," at Poggio Bustone

MEANWHILE, FRANCIS CHOSE RIETI AS HIS OWN mission district. From Terni, he followed the course of the River Velino, which brought him through a whole series of larger and smaller towns—Stroncone, Cantalice, Poggio Bustone, Greccio. Everywhere, he found—as the legends tell us—the fear of God and the love of God almost vanished, and the way of penitence abandoned and despised. The broad way, the way of the world, the way the three evil lusts urge people along, were thickly frequented—the lust of the flesh, lust of the eyes, and pride of the world had almost unlimited sway. To "block the wrong and endless way of lust" (Julian Speier) was therefore the constant, principal task for Francis. In the Valley of Rieti, the saint's preaching was in those early days regarded as an evangelization in the proper significance of the word—a conversion from heathenism to Christianity.

It was while engaged in this work that Francis, according to his biographers, was made certain of the forgiveness of his sins, the certainty of which may be said to have been absolutely necessary to carry out the work he was to do.

Five hundred meters high in the mountains above the town of Poggio Bustone, and a thousand meters above the plain, there is a cave to which Francis, true to his Assisi habits, liked to go for prayer. There in great loneliness and dead silence, where only a single bird twittered and a mountain book gurgled, Francis kneeled long hours on hard stone under a naked cliff. And if we want to really understand him we must follow him to this mountain cave.

There had been, and was still, a hermit, an evangelist, and a missionary in his makeup, and wherever he had set his feet were found these grottos and caves, these *eremi* and *ritiri*, where he'd withdraw. Carceri at Assisi, St. Urbano at Narni, Fonte Colombo at Rieti, Monte Casale at Borgo San Sepolcro, Celle at Cortona, le Coste at Nottiano, Soteano at Chiusi, La Verna in the valley of Casentino, all give widespread testimony that the spirit that inspired Francis of Assisi was none other than the one that, in the latest of the olden days, had inspired Benedict of Nursia, and the same which later, in the first of the modern days, was to inspire Ignatius of Loyola. Francis in Poggio Bustone or by Fonte Colombo is a side piece to Benedict in Sacro Speco by Subiaco, to Ignatius Loyola in the cave at Manresa. To all of them applies the same exhortation: "Pray and work," *ora et labora*. All three strove in the midst of the industry of Martha to have the devotion of Mary.

And in the cave at Poggio Bustone, Francis tried to have such an hour as that of Mary at the feet of the Crucified One. Perhaps he had already uttered the prayer that is first revealed to us in the later hours of his life, and which in all its comprehensive conciseness is given here: "Who are you, my dear Lord and God, and who am I, your miserable worm of a servant? My dearest Lord, I want to love you! My Lord and my God, I give you my heart and my body, and would wish, if I only knew how, to do still more for the love of you!"

There was a double abyss (as Angela of Foligno has called it) yawning in those lonely hours of prayer in front of Francis: the Divine Being's abyss of goodness and light, and opposed to it Francis's own abyss of sin and darkness. For who was he that he dared to be the road sign for humanity, and a master of disciples, he who only a few years earlier had been a child of the world among children of the world, a sinner among sinners? Who was he to dare to preach to others, to warn and guide others—he who was not worthy to take the holy and pure name of Jesus Christ into his impure mortal mouth? Then he thought of what he had been, of what he yet might be if God did not stand by him, for that danger was always within him. Then he thought next of what others thought of him, some who honored him, some who followed, and some who hated him. He didn't know where to hide for shame, and the words of the Apostle rang in his ears: "lest perhaps, when I have preached to others, I myself should become a castaway" (1 Cor. 9:27).

This humility raged in him like a lion that leaves nothing of his prey, but grinds the bones for the marrow. All torn up and annihilated, Francis cast himself on his face before God, who had made heaven and earth, the God who is all truth and holiness, and before whose omnipotence nothing can stand without complete truth and holiness. Francis looked into the depths of his being and saw that on the whole earth there was not to be found a more useless creature, a greater sinner, a soul more lost and fallen than himself, and from the depths of his need he groaned before God, "Lord, be merciful to me a poor sinner!"

And it happened that the empty cave over Poggio Bustone saw a miracle, one that always happens when a soul in complete distrust of itself calls out to God in confidence, hope, and clarity—then there comes to pass a great miracle of *justification*. "I fear everything from my badness, but from thy goodness I also hope for all"—that was the innermost meaning of the prayer Francis sent up to God. The answer came, as it always comes: "Fear not, my son, your sins are forgiven!"

From that hour, Francis was fully armed for the things that awaited him. He was drawn into the heart of Christianity.

(Book Two: Francis the Evangelist, *chapter 1)*

From various travel writings . . .

(These samples demonstrate more of the author's talent for description, and his passion for faith.)

THE PRIEST AT A VILLAGE IN OCCUPIED FLANDERS WAS called to a deathbed and set out with the Blessed Sacrament in a pyx on his breast. On the way he had to pass a bridge which was guarded by a German sentry. The priest had not had time to provide himself with a countersign, and consequently, the sentry refused to let him pass.

"And if I pass over all the same?" said the ecclesiastic.

"Then I have orders to shoot," was the answer.

"Very well, my friend," said the priest, "then shoot me when I come back!"

Then there was the story of the well-known Belgian publisher Dessain, arrested later for the transgression of having printed Cardinal Mercier's pastoral letter.[55] He rescued the Sacred Host from a burning church, and, pursued by the enemy, he held the Ciborium in his left hand while he steered his bicycle with his right. He rang his bell in every village he passed through, and the people knelt down to the God whom they beheld in flight on Dessain's bicycle, as once he fled to Egypt on Joseph's and Mary's ass.

(From "At Belgian Headquarters," The War Pilgrim, *72–73)*

---

55 Désiré Mercier, 1851–1926.

Y OU HAVE SEEN THERE ARE CARABINEERS TRAVELING by this train?" asked the Italian officer who, up to that moment, had not found me worth a remark, though he favored me with more looks of suspicion. We were in the train between Rapallo and Genoa, and were alone. I answered I *had* seen the carabineers. Impossible to deny it, as they had just passed along the corridor.

"Spies are arrested every day on this train," continued the young officer. I saw what he was driving at and showed my colors by handing him my card with my Italian address printed on it. This led to conversation. The young lieutenant, who seemed to be about twenty-five years old, had traveled a good deal and, like many of his generation, had studied in Germany. We compared notes on German cities and customs, and after a discussion on morals we arrived at the subject of religion.

"I am a Catholic, *Cattolico Apostolico Romano*," [56] said the dashing young officer, "but I must confess that before the war I had not much truck with religion. Then I went to the front, and there I learned to pray. Mass in the trenches is different from Mass at home, when the priest rattles off his Latin and a dirty altar-boy makes the responses, turning around in between to signal to his friends in the church. And the guns preach a better sermon than any Capuchin. When you have seen what I have seen—for instance, a shell falls among a group of four officers: when the smoke clears away, a heap of flesh remains, and from a tree hangs a newly torn leg, still

56 *Cattolico Apostolico Romano* = "Roman Catholic Apostolic." Apparently, this was printed on Jørgensen's business card.

warm—" The young officer fell silent. He had spoken in a curt and almost brutal way. Then he looked out the window. For a few minutes, he could not go on.

The line runs along the shores of the Genoese Riviera. Fishermen are dragging in their boats on the russet beach that runs down to the bluish-green sea. The deep Nervi gardens are full of flowers. Women are standing on doorsteps in the sunshine with babies in their arms. Here peace is still a reality. But the train rushes, rushes, rushes to the other reality, the great blood-red reality of the war.

As railway reading I have Ernest Psichari's *Le Voyage du Centurion*.[57] Ernest Psichari!—one knows from whom he descended by nature. He has the same baptismal name as his grandfather, Renan, whose *Vie de Jésus* is read as a novel—the Ernest Renan who, with Hippolyte Taine, is the brilliant French twin-star on the spiritual horizon of the middle of the last century: Ernest Renan and the daughter of the devout painter Ary Scheffer. The issue of the union between the renegade priest and the Calvinist woman was a daughter who, by a Greek father, gave birth to another Ernest. Renan died; and the new Ernest, Ernest Psichari, grew up and became a smart officer—such another as he who is reading in a corner of the compartment the latest issue of *Noi e il Mondo*.[58]

57 *The Centurion's Journey*. Psichari wrote this book while soldiering in the Sahara.
58 Ernest Psichari, 1883–1914, baptized Greek Orthodox, converted to Catholicism in 1913, then decided to join the Belgian army, to act on his faith, rather than enter the priesthood. He was killed in the Battle of the Frontiers.

But this young Frenchman did not wait for the guns to preach to him before he returned to the Church which his grandfather had left. In 1913, Lieutenant Ernest Psichari of the French Colonial Army, recently returned from Africa, wrote: "The young men of the present day have more moral backbone than those of the preceding generation. We are conscious of an appalling responsibility; we have an oppressive certainty, which never for a moment leaves us, of an overwhelming obligation. Our generation—I speak of those whose manhood began with the opening of the century—is full of significance. All hopes are centered in us, and we know it. On us depends the salvation of France, that is to say, of the world and civilization. Everything rests upon us." Written in 1912–13, the following words now read like prophecy: "It seems to me that the young men are dimly conscious that they will see great things, and that great things will be done through them. It will not fall to their lot to become amateurs or skeptics. They will not go through life like tourists. They know what is expected of them."

A certain set of the new generation, Psichari felt, is too much interested in sport. The word *intellectual*, he says, has almost become a term of abuse. . . . "Our dear Jacques Maritain" bears witness: "Supernatural understanding is the second of the gifts of the Holy Ghost. It is that for which the Psalmist pleads with such wondrous earnestness—*intellectum da mihi*. With the understanding we will one day behold God. Our intelligence is just as valuable to God as our heart, and in order to preserve it, he sent us nothing less than the peace that passes all understanding." This, say the young men of France, is the intelligence which the old intellectuals degraded. The young will watch over it as over their dearest.

In the desert, in solitude, beneath the immense blue and luminous star-lit night, the soldier meets another who, like himself, is not afraid of the absolute. They understand what ordinary people often do not, that freedom is the ideal of slaves. Those with noble hearts desire to obey. We, who were young in the century of disobedience, and whose plebian nature knew only one solution: "Emancipation!" should feel ashamed and edified at the sight of this new, young generation of nobility, whose ambition is to serve.

Ernest Psichari kneels on the desert sand beneath the infinite blue dome and makes his confession of faith: "Man needs God; Jesus gives God in giving Himself. Man needs holiness; Jesus comes and it stands revealed. Jesus is the balance of the world; He is the fulfillment of all that is human and all that is divine. He is the ring that was lacking, the marriage ring that joins the old covenant with the new. He is the meeting of man with God—the unique meeting, from which has sprung the spark of love."

"God, soul, immortality—good, old, somewhat rough words, which we have no objection to retaining, but to which we give a new meaning," wrote Ernest Renan once, and in all the haunts of Positivism and Free-thought heads were bowed in assent. The God Whom Ernest Psichari invokes in the Sahara is the old, plain-spoken God. "He is the Father Who loves us, Who desires that we should be free and happy. He is not a principle, or an idea, or a dogma. He is our Father and our Friend and our Brother. He is not a word or a chimera; He is One by Whom we are nourished."

("The Cross and the Sword," The Dublin Review, *Vol. 160, April 1917. Excerpts.)*

From

Catherine of Siena . . .

To be sincere, I must confess that, at first, I felt less in sympathy with Catherine of Siena than with Francis of Assisi. In the energetic nature of the Sienese saint there is somewhat of a domineering spirit, an element of tyranny that was repugnant to me. Her perpetual and very feminine *lo voglio*, "I will," is in absolute contrast to the gentle Umbrian who preferred to see his life work fail rather than make use of power and authority "like the Podestà of this world." This Catherine was never afraid to do, but that is why, I imagine, her last hour was less peaceful than that of Francis of Assisi. At the supreme moment doubts assailed her: conscience, which becomes a devil's advocate when the light of the world of truth begins to shine in the soul and eternity appears in all its overwhelming reality, whispered to her that the work of her whole life had been inspired only by obstinacy and vanity. He whom the hymn calls "*Franciscus pauper et humilis*" had no need to defend himself against such accusations.

My relations with Catherine therefore began, to tell the truth, under somewhat annoying conditions. At certain times, I was almost afraid of her. But gradually, as I began to know her more intimately, the same thing befell me that befell so many others during her earthly life—I was subjugated by her and had to acknowledge myself beaten. Like the Franciscan who had at first criticized her so violently, I, too, became a zealous *"Caterinato,"* and, like the woman in the fresco of Andrea di Vanni in the Cappella delle Volte, I, too, fell upon my knees, and with my lips humbly touched the pale hands which, though not outwardly showing any stigmata, were yet pierced by the pain of the Wounds of Christ.

(From the Preface)

When you step into the church of San Domenico in Siena, you see at once on the right side a door to a closed chapel, on a slightly higher level than the rest of the church. In earlier times this chapel was open, only some arches, traces of which can still be seen, separating it from the main nave. Steps lead up to it. When the arches were walled up, a couple of steps were left standing—they can be seen in a square opening in the wall, and an old inscription says: "Catherine mounted these steps to pray to Christ, her Bridegroom."

This chapel is the Capella delle Volte, mentioned again and again in the story of Catherine. Here the Mantellate held their meetings and here Catherine was clothed by Father Bartolommeo Montucci in the white habit, the belt, the black mantle, and the white coif in the presence of all the Sisters one Sunday morning in 1363. We are told by Raymond of Capua that when she came home from church that day, she said to herself: "Look, now you have entered into religion and it is not fitting that you should go on living as you have previously.

Your life in the world is over, a new life is beginning. The white robe you are wearing signifies that you must be girded with sheerest purity. The black cloak means that you must be completely dead to the world. And henceforth you must walk in the narrow path, walked by very few."

After she had been alone in her cell for quite some time, she had a beautiful and significant vision. It seemed to her that she beheld a large tree full of beautiful fruits. Round the foot of the tree there was a high and thick hedge of thorns, so that it was difficult to get inside to the tree and gather the fruit.

A short way off there was a little hill, thoroughly covered with corn already whitening to harvest. The corn looked very beautiful, but the ears were barren, and on being touched they crumbled away into dust. It seemed to her that many people came and passed by. They stopped opposite the tree, and desiring the fair fruit, they tried to get inside to it, but the thorns pricked them and they soon gave up trying to break through the hedge. Then they caught sight of the corn-covered hill nearby and ran up to it and ate of the unwholesome corn, which turned to dust between their fingers, making them ill and depriving them of their strength.

Then others came and had more courage than the first. They broke through the hedge, but when they reached the tree, saw that the fruit hung high up, and that the trunk of the tree was smooth and difficult to climb. They too, therefore, turned away and ate some of the corn, which only made them hungrier than they were before. At last some came some who both broke through the hedge and climbed the tree. They plucked the fruits and ate them, and were thereby strengthened in spirit, so that from that moment they had a loathing of all other food.

"But Catherine," Caffarini relates, "wondered why so many men and women could be so foolish and so blind, that they would follow and love the false and deceitful world, rather than surrender themselves to Jesus Christ, who calls us and invites us and who is faithful in all that he promises, even in this world consoling his servants and bestowing joy upon them. For that tree, she understood, signifies the eternal incarnate Word, and the ineffable fruits of the tree are all the virtues. The little hill, on the other hand, which does not yield good corn, but only husks, is the barren field of the world, which people till with great and fruitless toil. And they who give up trying to get into the tree as soon as they feel the thorns, are those who think they cannot endure a God-fearing life and give it up before they have tried it. The others, who lose courage when they see how tall the tree is, are those who begin with a good will and a good heart, but who weary after a while and do not persevere in their first resolve. The last kind are those who really believe and who remain steadfast in the truth."

In this vision, Catherine's fundamental view of life, which was to grow fuller and deeper with the coming years, was already given. Human beings are placed, she feels, between two powers, both of which appeal to their love. One of these two powers is truth, life, peace, happiness, and everlasting life. The other is delusion, the world, the ever enchanting and ever disappointing mirage of Satan. There are some who would maintain that this doctrine is Buddhist or ancient Greek, that it has come down from Shakyamuni or from Plato or Plotinus. It comes from the Gospels. It is to be found in the New Testament. It is the entirely firm conviction of primitive Christianity that there is an undying enmity between God and "the world," between the children of God and the children of the world. The disciples of Jesus are "not of the world," therefore the world hates them. Jesus, who prays for sinners, "does not pray for the world." Antichrist is "the prince of this world," the Christian faith "overcomes the world"; it is the duty of a Christian not to love the world, or the things that are in the world. Love of the world is the exact opposite of the love of God: "If anyone love the world, the love of God is not in him."

This evangelical and apostolic teaching has been faithfully preserved by the Catholic Church down through the ages (as the Catholic Church altogether is the unadulterated representative of genuine primitive Christian thought). It is Augustine's doctrine of "the two cities," it is the teaching of the Dominican mystic of "the two kinds of love," it is Ignatius of Loyola's teaching of "the two standards." "The soul that is endowed with reason becomes impure," writes St. Thomas Aquinas, "when it gives its love to temporal things and gives itself up to them." In wandering calmly through land after land, Henry Suso, the other Dominican and the spiritual kinsman of Aquinas, said that he might "draw loving hearts from temporal to eternal love," and "make them loathe mortal love and cherish that which is everlasting."

In human beings, everything issues from the heart and the heart is never inactive. "Neither the Creator nor the creature was ever without love," says Dante. We do not know whether Catherine had read Dante (he was read and treasured among her disciples), but she says in similar words: "The soul cannot live without loving." Everything then, depends on what we love, "for we must love either God or the world. And the soul always unites itself with that which it loves and is transformed by it."

(From Book I, chapter 6)

An Autobiography . . .

Early Experiences of Assisi

While Mogens was talking, we had by steadily ascending streets reached the higher part of Assisi, where the old, decayed church of San Lorenzo stands and where the pavement of the streets merges into the stony mountain. It was getting toward noon, the sun was hot, but the fresh breeze rarely absent from Assisi swept over the grass fields about the old ruined castle and brought us the scent of flowering thyme. From the height, we looked down into the valley of the Tescio, where the river flows green deep down between violent rocks. Then the clocks in the towers of the cathedral and the town hall struck twelve in the town below us, and from all the great and small towers in Assisi the Angelus bells pealed.

A single frail little bell was the first to begin, far too soon, like a school child eager to show what he can do. Not for long, however, did it ring alone; one-by-one they all joined in, all the silver bells of Assisi, all the golden bells of Assisi, all the clear crystal bells of Assisi, all the booming and clanging doom-day bells of Assisi, all the joyous, bright, happy, exulting and blissful heavenly bells of Assisi. From the extreme north to the furthest south of Assisi the sound runs like a fire in grass. Everywhere the clear tones soar like bright flames in the air. Santa Chiara rings out below Pincio. San Francesco answers from far away in the Colle dell'Inferno. San Pietro and Santa Maria del Vescovado peal long and exultingly, San Rufino rings deeply and soberly. Santa Maria sopra Minerva, San Quirico, Sant'Apollinare, Chiesa Nuova, Francescuccio, the church of the Capuchins, the chapel of the Colettines, the convent of the German nuns, Sant'Andrea, Santa Margherita—all the high towers and all the small belfries, in which one sees the bells swinging in and out, all of them ring, all of them chime, all of them rejoice, all of them play before the Lord and praise His holy Mother: *Ave Maria, gratia plena.* "Hail, Mary, full of grace, blessed art thou among women, and blessed is the fruit of thy womb, Jesus!"

I turned to Mogens to express what I felt. He was standing with bared head in the sunshine, his face hidden in his hands. I understood that he was praying.

(Vol. 1, pp. 241–42)

Immediately after my arrival in Assisi the great feast of indulgences at Portiuncula was celebrated on the first and second of August. We took part in it: he [Mogens Ballin] as one of the faithful, I as a spectator, first up at San Francesco's in Assisi, afterwards down in the large, light pilgrimage church of Santa Maria degli Angeli, which is built over the Portiuncula chapel.

We spent almost the whole of the first day there: first, in the church where the pilgrims came in a steady stream through the porch which has inscribed above it, "*Haec est porta vitae aeternae*";[59] then, outside among the market booths, purchasing naïve woodcuts of St. Francis and St. Clare, buying rosaries and medals for Ballin's Catholic friends, buying small crosses of mother-of-pearl from Naples, with the picture of the saint of Assisi carved roughly in the silvery bright surface. We had lunch at the tables, above which were poles with whole roasted pigs hanging, slices being sold for pennies. We ate our meal standing among unshaved peasants and women with gaily colored blouses. We refreshed ourselves afterwards with a huge slice of watermelon, rosy pink, full of black seeds, delicious to look at—"but it tastes like the smell of washing-day," said Mogens.

Then he explained to me what indulgences meant, speaking also of Confession and the Sacrament of the altar. "Christ," he said, "made use of all the forms and thoughts at hand—in baptism, for instance, and in the Holy Supper. Both are Jewish customs that he developed further. The idea of an 'eaten god' is also found among Hindus and Persians, in Greek mysteries and African religions. These myths, this superstition, if you like, prepared the way for the truth, made the Christian dogma easy to understand, easy to accept." It was evident that he was well-informed, and I had no fault to find with his teaching.

We then saw together the miraculous rose bush, and I

59 Latin inscribed above the entrance to the Portiuncula: "This is the gate to eternal life."

did not object when my friend told me the roses haven't had thorns since the night when St. Francis, to overcome temptation, threw himself naked into it, and that its leaves are still stained as though with his blood.

Deeply impressed, I saw the pilgrims from southern Italy set out on their return homeward, with their large crucifix in front of them. Carrying their tall cross-headed staffs they walked away backwards, singing, toward the little chapel in which they had obtained forgiveness of their sins, and which they wanted to see as long as they could. *"Evviva Maria! Maria evviva!"*[60] And for once, only once, my Protestantism not daring more, I followed my friend on his path through Portiuncula, where the silver hearts gleamed from the bare walls and the golden flames of the candles on the altar stood motionless in an atmosphere of burning silence. Only once through the chapel, between kneeling and prostrate figures upon which one almost trod. Only one genuflection to the altar glimpsed behind the wrought-iron screen, against which the closely thronged, silent, motionless figures were at prayer. Then, out of the chapel, out of the stream of pilgrims, out of the church.

A strange peace settled on me as we walked together up the road from Santa Maria degli Angeli to Assisi. It was near sunset—up there stood the church and convent of the saint, golden yellow, as though carved out of old ivory or wrought in beaten gold. Up there stood the town of the saint, rose pink and violet in the glow of the setting sun, its old houses and its

60 "Hurray, Mary! Mary, hurray!"

churches and convents rising in terrace above terrace like a vine-covered hill. There was the mountain of the saint, Monte Subasio with Carceri in its wooded glen, and at the foot, among the olive trees, San Damiano. In the evening light, the huge dome of the mountain was mauve and pink with blood-red streaks that were stony paths or furrows formed by rain torrents. "This is the city that is set on a hill and that cannot be hid," I said to Mogens. In the evening when I was alone in my room, from which I looked out across Umbria and heard the murmur of Fonte Olivieri in the street below, I wrote in my diary: "It has been years since I have felt such happiness as I do this day. Lord, Lord, I thank you and praise you with all my poor heart!"

(Vol. 1, pp. 256–58)

On Bruges and Béguines

At first Bruges did not make any deep impression upon me. I arrived in pouring rain, put up at a small hotel, and at once went out. The streets seemed to me to be far too modern, and the marketplace, which I soon reached, was likewise, despite the town hall and the huge tower. As the rain continued pouring, I sought refuge in a small tavern where the waitress smelled of patchouli said, "Yes," and flirted in a corner with a regular. Outside, the rain poured in torrents. It grew darker and darker. The marketplace lay glistening wet, violet, crossed by dark wayfarers. Against a violet sky the belfry rose black. There was a sonorous ringing up above, but so remote as though smothered in the rainy mist. Further away other chimes answered and I saw a Gothic spire—it must have been that of the cathedral, Saint-Sauveur.

I drank my weak ale, heard the scented girl giggling in the corner, looked out at the deserted marketplace, where the lamps gave a feeble light, and caught a glimpse of a bandstand. It was one of those moments when life becomes so weirdly real and reality so unspeakably sad—when eternity rings so remotely, so high up, like half-smothered chimes, and down here there is only weak ale if one is poor, strong ale if one has money.

This mood of oppression was still upon me the next morning when I went out to see Bruges. In vain I kneeled in the cathedral by the gilded shrine of Charles the Good. I felt that I ought to pray there for Denmark, pray for the return of my country to the true faith—and I could not. Dull and deaf I went to St. John's Hospital, to the church of Our Lady, to the museum in pottery and the civic museum. I had an introduction to a young government official and writer, Dr. Axters, but I was careful not to call upon him—not until late in the afternoon when the spell was broken and the bandage of indifference had fallen from my eyes and I *saw* Bruges.

It happened on the bridge leading over to the *Béguinage*. In my lethargic state I stopped there and gazed up the canal. There are gardens on either side and green shrubs beneath high, dark walls and houses. Large, blossoming elder bushes lean out from one of these little gardens (it was June); full-branched willow trees dip their long tresses in the water. A little further along, I saw another bridge, other houses, walls, gables, then the soaring tower of the church of Our Lady. The water was smooth, without a single ripple, with large flakes of green. Swallows were darting noiselessly over it, in under the bridge and back again. An old woman in the black Bruges cloak, with the hood drawn up over the white coif, came up toward me, passed by, walked down the other side, through the gate of the *Béguinage*. As though wakened out of a trance, I followed her, saw above the gateway a statue of Saint Elisabeth of Thuringia, and in the vaulted roof of the gateway a large, old crucifix, solemn and full of pain, which I saluted.

I came into the large green in the middle of the *Béguinage*. It is intersected by paths running lengthwise and crosswise; a great many tall elms sigh in the faint breeze. Round about the green stand the small houses of the *Béguines*. They are all white with green doors and green-painted window frames and crossbars, and they have red or brown tiled roofs.

I still follow my guide, who crosses over to the church at one side of the large green. I follow her inside—a large, light, handsome Renaissance church in a pure style. Here and there a few *Béguines* are already kneeling on the rush-seated prie-dieux; they are dressed like my guide in the black Spanish mantilla with white coifs about their calm, peaceful faces. I too find a prie-dieu and kneel down. A good-looking, half-grown altar boy comes in and lights the candles on the high altar; a priest enters, opens the tabernacle, and exposes the Blessed

Sacrament. Up in the tower a bell rings some short strokes; I hear the *Béguines* coming in behind me, more and still more; at last I am quite surrounded by black cloaks and white coifs. Up at the altar the incense rises toward the monstrance, and over my bowed head ascend the clear voices of women singing *O salutaris Hostia. . . .*[61]

And as prayers follow singing and singing follows prayers, the Litany of the Sacred Hearts is said in strong, sincere, and hearty Flemish—and after *O salutaris* they sing *Tantum ergo*—the supernatural rises up anew before me in its beauty, its grandeur, and its strength. I feel that my lot is cast, that my choice is made forever, and that I have chosen the better part which shall not be taken away from me.

The thralldom was over—the petrification destroyed. The next morning, I went to Mass in the chapel of the Precious Blood, built in the Middle Ages as a magnificent shrine for the linen shroud stained with the blood of Christ and brought home from the Holy Land. The treasured relic is always exposed on a sort of pulpit; everyone can approach and kiss the glass covering the blood-stained linen. All through the morning Mass is said in the chapel. After the last Mass, Benediction is given with the relic while all the people kneel. The censers swing right up and stand up vertically in the acolyte's hands.

---

61 Part of a Catholic Eucharistic hymn, written by St. Thomas Aquinas in the thirteenth century. "O saving Victim. . . ." This may have been the office of Lauds on the Feast of Corpus Christi. *Tantum ergo*, "Therefore so great," which is mentioned a few sentences later, is another hymn by Aquinas.

From La Chapelle du Saint-Sang I went to the Jerusalem church, in the crypt of which a Flemish Crusader had caused a reproduction of the Holy Sepulchre to be built, and in the church of Our Lady I stood before the Madonna of Michelangelo, a sister to the Pietà in St. Peter's, and wrote in my diary: "Michelangelo portrayed man as he issued from the hand of the Middle Ages. What beauty, nobility, fineness, gentle grace there is in his Mary! And into what has man been transformed by the later centuries?"

(Vol. 2, pp. 196–99)

On Léon Bloy[62]

I have mentioned the part which Bloy played for me as a tutor in uncompromising controversy and as a literary model generally. I have said nothing about my personal connection with him, and will only briefly touch upon it here. It was early in the spring of 1899 that I received a letter in which the French writer whom I admired so much informed me that he was living in Kolding, that he intended to pitch his tent in his wife's country (Madame Jeanne Bloy was a daughter of the poet Molbech), and that he hoped to have an opportunity of making my personal acquaintance. At the same time, I received from him a copy of his latest book,

62 Léon Bloy, 1846–1917, French novelist, essayist, and poet; Catholic convert and apologist; an influence on Graham Greene, John Irving, Pope Francis, many others; frequently credited by Jacques and Raïssa Maritain for showing the way to Catholicism.

Le Mendiant ingrate, which made a deep impression on me by its description of the author's poverty.[63] Here Bloy had touched a string which found a deep response in me, and in my little weekly paper I wrote a long article about the book, about Bloy's work as a whole, and finally about the straitened circumstances in which he was living, and what had now compelled him to seek refuge in Denmark.

Bloy was grateful to me for this article, which I followed up with some chapters of *Le Mendiant ingrate* in a translation. Several Copenhagen Catholics interested themselves in him and sent him some pecuniary assistance. And between him and myself a correspondence began, which unfortunately is no longer in my possession. On my part, it was characterized by a pupil's admiration; on his, by the mature artist's absolute mastery of the French language. I remember that in one of his first letters he reproached me for having said in my essay about him (written in 1894 in La Rocca) that he was "not entirely orthodox." I could not offend him more deeply, he asserted. Nevertheless, we were on very good terms by letter, and before I left Denmark in 1899 to go to Assisi for the second time, he asked me to pay him a visit in Kolding.

This visit lasted twenty-four hours, and I returned home with an impression which I can best characterize as complete disorientation. I was bewildered, and did not know what to believe or think. I found in Bloy a certain jovial bonhomie

---

63 Christian Molbech, 1783-1857, Danish critic, historian, poet; professor at the University of Copenhagen; a contemporary of Søren Kierkegaard. *Le Mendiant ingrate*, "The Ungrateful Beggar," contained journal entries of the author, published in 1898.

which I liked and tried to keep to, but other sides of his character frightened, even appalled, me.

A year later, Bloy returned my visit in Copenhagen. As in Kolding, my first feeling was of filial affection and a pupil's reverence for a master. Bloy said excellent things, striking things, inspiring things; he was a virtuoso in telling pathetic and seizing traits of Christian heroism. He had the gift of tears and could draw tears from others. I will never forget his description of the French missionary in remote India who, from the ship onward, which sailed up one of the great rivers, proclaimed the hour of Mass by the blowing of a conch shell, and from the primeval forest came his parishioners, plunging in the water and swimming out to the ship, "like crocodiles, whose prey is Jesus Christ." Bloy was a master in producing violent emotions, and his criticism, which was as hard as a hammer, crushed where it fell. But I could not help him in smashing Thorvaldsen into bits, and I revolted when he declared about Leo XIII—whose Christian democracy he disliked—"I loathe that Pope!"[64]

We parted more coolly than we had met. After a stay of seventeen months in Denmark, Bloy returned to France. While I was in Belgium in 1901 I received an issue of the *Mercure de France,* in which he published an extremely

---

64 Bertel Thorvaldsen, 1770–1844, great Danish sculptor, the only non-Catholic to produce a work for St. Peter's Basilica. Leo XIII, Pope from 1878–1903. Bloy was probably upset by the Pope's encyclical *Rerum novarum,* in which he argued for the rights of workers: fair wages, collective bargaining, etc., at a time when the Industrial Age was at full swing, and exploitation of workers had become common in the modern world.

favorable, brilliantly written article about me. Simultaneously, I received a letter in which he asked me to come from Brussels to Paris to see him. I declined this invitation with thanks, and then a long time passed when I did not hear from him.

Then came word from a disciple—someone who, like me, had come under the magic of the great artist in words, and been bewitched by his violent religion—writing to me to say that Léon Bloy had broken with me. The reason was that in an article in *Vort Land* about French prose of the present day I had omitted to mention him, although I had mentioned Villiers de l'Isle-Adam and Barbey d'Aurevilly, and "these names cried despairingly for the name of Léon Bloy." The punishment for this transgression was the forfeiture of his friendship.

"It is dangerous to have learned Christianity from Léon Bloy," I wrote in my diary after his visit to Copenhagen. And if he sought me out, wouldn't it be because I was one of his family? I took the dismissal now as a good omen. I did not judge Bloy, but I understood that he was harmful to me and that it was not without peril for me to walk in his paths.

I did not judge Bloy. I do not judge him. I continue to admire him as an admirable prose writer, and to honor that unyieldingness with which he has carried out his program of life. Never has he written a line to please any public, never withheld a judgment for the sake of avoiding a breach. He has accepted never to obtain success and never to receive appreciation, other than that of a small circle of the initiated. When I saw him in Denmark he was already looking like an old man; he must now be over seventy and he goes on living, goes on writing, goes on working and having influence. New young men are continually drawing near him, are impressed, fascinated, influenced, converted, and he counts among his friends not only poets, men of letters and musicians (Emile Baumann, Edmond Barthelemy, Vincent d'Indy), but also a philosopher like Jacques Maritain, a natural scientist like Pierre Termier.

Fifteen years have passed since Léon Bloy said goodbye to me, but though I am no longer among those who receive his works with one of those masterful dedications, I think I have read everything he has written. Wherever I happen to be in the world—when I see Bloy's name on the cover of a new book in a bookseller's window, I must go in and buy the book! And through three hundred pages I am again under the old magic. I grow enthusiastic, I hate, I love, I revolt, I am angered, I glow, I melt, I weep—"all the feelings that slept in the crypts of the heart break out of their hiding place and crowd together like a company of mutilated virgins, naked, blind, hungry and sobbing" (*Le Mendiant ingrate*).

I said goodbye to Léon Bloy—and surrendered myself to Francis of Assisi.

(Vol. 2, pp. 235–38)

EDITOR'S NOTES AND ACKNOWLEDGMENTS

I have occasionally slightly altered the originally published translations. This is not to suggest that I read Danish—only that I have at times exchanged what were common English words, expressions, and idioms of a century ago with similar but different ones that are more common today. I think both author and translator would approve, for instance, of such changes in the opening paragraph of *Pilgrim Walks in Franciscan Italy*: "of great antiquity" to "of time immemorial," and "days of yore" to "days gone by"—and in the second paragraph of the same work, "Finally" for "At length," and "valley" for "vale." Later, and throughout, "Occasionally" for "Now and again"; "Then" for "Presently"; and so on. Similar alterations have been made to the other books. I also occasionally divided a long paragraph into two, added commas and removed semicolons, and, in the case of *Pilgrim Walks*, broke a long chapter into two. Thank you to Fr. Stephanos Pedrano, OSB, monk and priest of Prince of Peace Abbey in California for help with one particular Latin translation.

ABOUT PARACLETE PRESS

WHO WE ARE

As the publishing arm of the Community of Jesus, Paraclete Press presents a full expression of Christian belief and practice—from Catholic to Evangelical, from Protestant to Orthodox, reflecting the ecumenical charism of the Community and its dedication to sacred music, the fine arts, and the written word. We publish books, recordings, sheet music, and video/DVDs that nourish the vibrant life of the church and its people.

WHAT WE ARE DOING

BOOKS | PARACLETE PRESS BOOKS show the richness and depth of what it means to be Christian. While Benedictine spirituality is at the heart of who we are and all that we do, our books reflect the Christian experience across many cultures, time periods, and houses of worship.

We have many series, including *Paraclete Essentials*; *Paraclete Fiction*; *Paraclete Poetry*; *Paraclete Giants*; and for children and adults, *All God's Creatures*, books about animals and faith; and *San Damiano Books*, focusing on Franciscan spirituality. Others include *Voices from the Monastery* (men and women monastics writing about living a spiritual life today), *Active Prayer*, and new for young readers: *The Pope's Cat*. We also specialize in gift books for children on the occasions of Baptism and First Communion, as well as other important times in a child's life, and books that bring creativity and liveliness to any adult spiritual life.

The MOUNT TABOR BOOKS series focuses on the arts and literature as well as liturgical worship and spirituality; it was created in conjunction with the Mount Tabor Ecumenical Centre for Art and Spirituality in Barga, Italy.

MUSIC | PARACLETE PRESS DISTRIBUTES RECORDINGS of the internationally acclaimed choir *Gloriæ Dei Cantores*, the *Gloriæ Dei Cantores Schola*, and the other instrumental artists of the *Arts Empowering Life Foundation*.

PARACLETE PRESS IS THE EXCLUSIVE NORTH AMERICAN DISTRIBUTOR for the Gregorian chant recordings from St. Peter's Abbey in Solesmes, France. Paraclete also carries all of the Solesmes chant publications for Mass and the Divine Office, as well as their academic research publications.

In addition, PARACLETE PRESS SHEET MUSIC publishes the work of today's finest composers of sacred choral music, annually reviewing over 1,000 works and releasing between 40 and 60 works for both choir and organ.

VIDEO | Our video/DVDs offer spiritual help, healing, and biblical guidance for a broad range of life issues including grief and loss, marriage, forgiveness, facing death, understanding suicide, bullying, addictions, Alzheimer's, and Christian formation.

LEARN MORE ABOUT US AT OUR WEBSITE:
WWW.PARACLETEPRESS.COM
OR PHONE US TOLL-FREE AT 1.800.451.5006

SCAN
TO
READ
MORE

YOU MAY ALSO BE INTERESTED IN THESE FROM SAN DAMIANO BOOKS...

Francis in His Own Words
The Essential Writings

Translated by Jon M. Sweeney

ISBN 978-1-64060-019-5
Trade paperback | $16.99

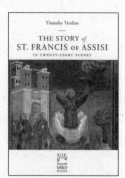

The Story of St. Francis of Assisi
In Twenty-Eight Scenes

Timothy Verdon

ISBN 978-1-64060-424-7
Trade paperback | $24.99

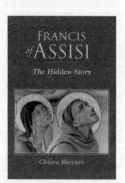

Francis of Assisi
The Hidden Story

Chiara Mercuri

ISBN 978-1-64060-275-5
Trade paperback | $23.00